FOR UPDATES, RECENT NEWS, & OTHER RESOURCES ... SEE OUR WEB SITE AT:

www.smart-publications.com

You will find:

- *A subscription offer to our free e-newsletter*

- *The latest facts and findings on the low-carb anti-aging diet*

- *A complete catalog of all our health enhancement books*

- *A directory of healthcare practitioners knowledgeable in alternative medicine*

- *Many other articles you may find of great interest and value*

SMART PUBLICATIONS™
Your Source For Alternatives

Other Books From
SMART PUBLICATIONS™

Smart Drugs & Nutrients
by Ward Dean, M.D., and John Morgenthaler
Smart Publications™ (formerly Health Freedom
Publications) 1990
ISBN: 0-9627418-9-2

Smart Drugs II: The Next Generation
by Ward Dean, M.D., John Morgenthaler, and Steven Wm.
Fowkes
Smart Publications™ (formerly Health Freedom
Publications) 1993
ISBN: 0-9627418-7-6

Better Sex Through Chemistry
by John Morgenthaler and Dan Joy
Smart Publications™ 1994
ISBN: 0-9627418-2-5

Natural Hormone Replacement
for Women Over 45
by Jonathan V. Wright, M.D. and John Morgenthaler
Smart Publications™ 1997
ISBN: 0-9627418-0-9

GHB: The Natural Mood Enhancer
by Ward Dean, M.D., John Morgenthaler,
and Steven Wm. Fowkes
Smart Publications™ 1998
ISBN: 0-9627418-6-8

5-HTP: The Natural Alternative to Prozac®
by John Morgenthaler and Lane Lenard, Ph.D.
Smart Publications™ 1998
ISBN: 0-9627418-4-1

Maximize Your Vitality & Potency for Men Over 40
by Jonathan V. Wright, M.D., and Lane Lenard, Ph.D.
Smart Publications™ 1999
ISBN: 0-9627418-1-7

The Smart Guide to Andro
by Lane Lenard, Ph.D.
Smart Publications™ 1999
ISBN: 0-9627418-5-X

The Smart Guide to Better Sex
by John Morgenthaler and Mia Simms
Smart Publications™ 1999
ISBN:1-890572-01-2

The Smart Guide to the Low-Carb Anti-Aging Diet
by John Morgenthaler and Mia Simms
Smart Publications™ 2000
ISBN: 1-890572-00-4

THE SMART GUIDE™ TO

Low-Carb Cooking

by Mia Simms

SMART PUBLICATIONS™
PO Box 4667
Petaluma, CA 94955

fax: 707 763 3944
www.smart-publications.com

The Smart Guide to Low-Carb Cooking

by Mia Simms

Published by:
Smart Publications™
PO Box 4667
Petaluma, CA 94955

fax: 707 763 3944
www.smart-publications.com

Library of Congress Catalog Card Number: 99-066639
First Printing 2000
Printed in the United States of America
First Edition

ISBN:1-890572-05-5 $12.95   Softcover

Warning - Disclaimer

Table of Contents

"No, that most certainly is **not** what is meant by a low-carb diet!"

Introduction

As a companion to the *Low-Carb Anti-Aging Diet*, this cookbook is filled with delicious and satisfying low-carbohydrate recipes. It features many powerful superfoods such as tofu, whey protein concentrate (WPC), vegetables and berries, along with "Fats to Grow Lean By," such as oil from fish, flax and coconuts (try the delicious and fat-burning Coconut-Flax "Butter").

Many of the items in this cookbook give you the opportunity to utilize health-promoting foods and fats addressed in the LCAA Diet, while others are designed to give you healthy alternatives to sugar-sweet foods and beverages you might otherwise miss on a low carbohydrate diet.

Here are some helpful tips:

- Keep a carbohydrate counter on hand. Maintain ketosis by staying within your personal best carbohydrate level. For most, this ranges between 30 and 60 carbohydrates per day. Ideally these should come from low-carb, high-nutrient vegetables and occasional small portions of fruit (berries).

- Keep a good supply of stevia on hand. Stevia is a non-caloric herbal sweetener that can be found at most health food stores or by mail order. It is more than 200 times sweeter than sugar and does not have the toxic effects of other non-caloric (artificial) sweeteners. All recipes in this cookbook utilize the stevia white extract produced by NOW Foods. If you cannot find it in your health food store, contact NOW Foods Inc. to locate the nearest retailer (see Resources).

- Some recipe ingredients, such as Bragg Liquid Aminos, Designer (whey) Protein and flax oil may be new to you. These can be purchased at most health or natural food stores. In case you are unable find them, we have listed company address/phone numbers in the Resources section.

- Choose organic* foods whenever possible. These are free of pesticides, herbicides and fungicides, as well as other chemicals used in growing — it truly is worth hunting them down and paying a little more. They also taste better and are nutritionally better. Take the taste test and find out how much better they taste and feel.

- Make sure to keep certain staples on hand, including soy flour, whey protein concentrate, flax oil, coconut oil and stevia. Check the shopping list in the appendix for more suggestions.

- Celtic salt is a mineral-rich sea salt that tastes better and is healthier than commercial varieties.

---

* In addition to organic produce, you can now purchase organic (or free-range) meat, poultry, eggs and dairy products.

- In recipes calling for garlic, be sure to cut, mince or press garlic about 10 minutes before adding it to your dish. This converts the amino acid alliin into a potent antibacterial enzyme called allinase. For a flavor enhancement, add garlic to your dish toward the end of the cooking process.

- In recipes that call for rice vinegar, check the label to make sure the product is unsweetened.

The following equipment will help in both food preparation and in saving time:

- a blender
- food processor
- non-stick skillet(s)

- double boiler and
- a wok (or large skillet)

The recipes in this cookbook include many of my favorites. As you explore cooking them and creating your own variations, you will be pleased at how easy it is to eat low carbohydrate. You'll also find that your favorite main dishes are easy to modify, since most of them are based on protein and vegetables. Baking is the most challenging, but it is possible with a variety of low carb "flours" on the market.

For consistent results, we recommend the following quality products, which are available in most health and natural product stores. If you cannot find them, please check Appendix B (Resources) for contact information:

Barlean's High Quality Organic Flax Oil
Bragg Liquid Aminos
Next Nutrition: Designer Protein (whey protein concentrate [WPC])
Now Foods Inc.: Quality stevia extract

The Grain and Salt Society (mineral-rich **Celtic Ocean Sea Salt**)
Spectrum Organic Coconut Oil
Thai Kitchen for Products (coconut milk, low carb condiments)

Food is meant to impart both pleasure and nutrition. We hope you find that the recipes here will also be used to delay aging, retain your good looks and vitality, and prevent diseases. Most of the recipes are fun, fast and fresh. Please refer to the *Low Carb Anti-Aging* book to review the importance of phytochemical and whey- and soy- enriched recipes found here.

You'll notice how many recipes call for the superfoods and health-promoting fats and oils detailed in the LCAA Diet. They include soya foods, whey protein concentrate, flax oil, coconut oil, cold water fish and an abundance of fresh vegetables and berries.

You will also find healthy alternatives to standards like mayonnaise, bread, margarine (flax-coconut "butter") and even hot chocolate!

Breakfasts

German Pancakes

2 eggs
2 tablespoons cream
2 tablespoons seltzer water
1/8 cup soy flour
1 pinch stevia
1/2 teaspoon baking soda
Coconut oil

Beat eggs, cream, seltzer, soy flour and soda by hand or in blender until thoroughly combined. Melt coconut oil in medium non-stick skillet on medium-low heat. Add half of the pancake mix and cook until underside turns a light golden brown. Flip pancake only once and remove from heat when both sides are done and add remaining batter to cook the second pancake.

Serve immediately, topped with a dollop of stevia-sweetened sour cream.
Serves 2

Carbs per recipe: 2
Carbs per serving: 1

Finnish Pancakes

3 eggs
1/2 cup cream
1/3 cup whey protein concentrate
2 tablespoons soy flour, sifted
1/2 teaspoon baking soda
2 tablespoons butter, melted
1 generous pinch stevia
Butter

Beat eggs and cream. Mix whey protein concentrate, soy flour, baking soda and stevia. Stir dry ingredients into egg mixture. Add melted butter and stir until smooth. Pour batter into a buttered, ovenproof skillet. Bake at 350 for 20 minutes or until toothpick comes out clean.

Serve sprinkled with stevia, cinnamon or low-carb strawberry syrup.
Serves 2

Carbs per recipe: 7
Carbs per serving: 4

Cottage Pancakes

2 eggs
1/3 cup cottage cheese
2 tablespoons sour cream
1/3 cup whey protein concentrate
1/8 cup soy flour
1 teaspoon baking powder
1 pinch stevia
Coconut oil

Beat eggs, cottage cheese and sour cream until well blended. In a separate bowl, mix soy flour, whey protein concentrate, baking powder and stevia. Gradually add dry ingredients to egg mixture and beat until thoroughly blended. Melt coconut oil in a medium-sized, non-stick skillet over medium heat. Pour about 1/6 of batter per pancake and cook until edges set and bubbles form. Flip pancakes once and remove from heat when both sides are done.

Serve with strawberry jam or syrup.
Serves 2

Carbs per recipe: 6
Carbs per serving: 3

Strawberry Syrup

1 1/2 teaspoons gelatin
3/4 cup purified water
1 cup fresh or frozen strawberries (unsweetened)
1/8 teaspoon stevia

Dissolve gelatin in cool water. Warm water and gelatin over low heat until gelatin dissolves completely. Place strawberries in a blender or food processor. Pour gelatin water over berries and blend until smooth. If using frozen berries, syrup will thicken nicely while blending. Keep unused portion in refrigerator.

Makes about 1 1/2 cups
(12 two-tablespoon servings)

Carbs per recipe: 13
Carbs per serving: 1

Strawberry Jam

2 cups fresh strawberries, washed and sliced
3 tablespoons lemon juice
1/8 teaspoon stevia extract
1/4 cup purified water
1 packet unflavored gelatin

Place strawberries, lemon juice and stevia in a medium-sized saucepan. Simmer mixture over medium heat for about five minutes or until berries soften and release their natural juices. Empty gelatin packet into a food processor or blender. Pour hot liquid only (not berries) over gelatin and blend on pulse until gelatin is completely dissolved.

Place in glass jar, cover and refrigerate. Jam is best when used within two weeks.

Makes about two cups
(16 2-tablespoon servings)

Carbs per recipe: 29
Carbs per serving: 2

French Toast

2 eggs
1/8 cup cream
1/8 cup purified water
1/2 teaspoon vanilla
1 pinch stevia
6 slices "Pound Cake" (see Breads & Desserts)
Coconut oil

Beat eggs in a small bowl. Add cream, water, vanilla and stevia; beat until smooth. Place "Pound Cake" slices in a shallow pan and pour French toast batter over them. Melt coconut oil in a large skillet over medium heat. Arrange bread slices evenly in skillet and cook until golden brown. Flip once, cook the other side and serve with cinnamon
Serves 2

Carbs per recipe: 19
Carbs per serving: 10

Simple poached eggs

Poached eggs are perfect for those who prefer a simple breakfast. They also lend themselves to some delicious gourmet variations (see below).

4 large eggs
Purified water

Place a large non-stick skillet over medium heat and pour in enough water to bring the level about one and a half inches. After water is brought to a gentle simmer, carefully break eggs into a small bowl and ease them into the water. Reduce heat to low and cook eggs about three minutes or until whites are firm. Remove eggs with a slotted spoon and serve.
Serves 2

Carbs per recipe: 2
Carbs per serving: 1

Variations: Serve poached eggs Benedict style or with steamed spinach and cheese, with hollandaise sauce (see sauces), chives or with other creative low-carb embellishments. Or you can even serve them Mexican style (next recipe).

Mexicana Breakfast

4 eggs, poached
1/4 cup chunky salsa
1/3 cup cheddar cheese, shredded
1/3 cup avocado, cut into chunks
2 tablespoons sour cream
2 tablespoons olives, sliced
2 tablespoons fresh cilantro, finely chopped

While eggs are poaching, heat salsa in microwave or over medium-low heat until hot but not simmering. Place eggs in a rimmed serving plate and top with warm salsa, shredded cheese, avocado chunks, sour cream, olives and fresh cilantro.
Serves 2

Carbs per recipe: 14
Carbs per serving: 7

Gourmet Egg Scramble

I discovered these before I was aware of the importance of low-carbohydrate eating. With no milk (and only cream) on hand, the result was creamy, fluffy, gourmet scrambled eggs.

4 eggs
2 tablespoons cream
1 tablespoon butter

Beat eggs and cream until evenly blended. Melt butter in a medium-sized skillet over medium-low heat. When butter begins to bubble (but not brown), pour egg mixture into the skillet. As the eggs are cooking, lift underneath them occasionally to allow uncooked eggs to make contact with the hot skillet. Serve when eggs are sufficiently cooked (do not allow them to brown).
Serves 2

Carbs per recipe: 3
Carbs per serving: 2

Variations: top with shredded cheese, sour cream or chives.

Egg Scramble

An excellent way to start the day.

2 eggs
1 tablespoon cream
1/2 cup your meat of choice or soft tofu, crumbled
1 pinch turmeric
1 pinch Celtic salt
1 tablespoon butter

Beat eggs and cream until evenly blended. Mix meat or crumbled tofu into egg mixture. Add turmeric and salt and stir well. Melt butter in a medium-sized skillet over medium-low heat. When butter begins to bubble (but not brown), pour egg mixture into the skillet. As mixture is cooking, lift underneath to occasionally allow uncooked portion to flow onto heated area. Serve when eggs are done.
2 servings

Carbs per recipe: 5 with tofu, 2 with meat
Carbs per serving: 3 or 1

Curds and Whey with Fresh Strawberries

For a refreshing variation, try this light and deliciously sweet breakfast.

1/2 cup cottage cheese
1/3 cup fresh strawberries, sliced
2 tablespoons whey protein concentrate
1 tablespoon pecan pieces, toasted

Slice fresh berries over cottage cheese in a mixing bowl. Sprinkle with whey protein concentrate and toasted pecan pieces.
Serves 1

Carbs per recipe: 11
Carbs per serving: 11

Poached Eggs Over Vegetables

1 tablespoon coconut oil
1/4 cup onion, sliced
1/2 cup mushrooms, sliced
1 cup broccoli, chopped
1/2 teaspoon salt
1/4 cup red pepper, diced
1 cup fresh spinach, shopped
1 teaspoon fresh basil
1/4 cup sour cream
4 eggs
Paprika to taste

Melt coconut oil in a large skillet over medium heat. Add onion and sauté until translucent. Add mushrooms, broccoli and salt. Stir-fry mixture for five minutes. Add red pepper and cook for five more minutes. Turn heat to medium-high and add spinach, basil and sour cream. In the meantime poach eggs in a separate saucepan. After five minutes, divide vegetables onto two plates and top each one with two poached eggs. Sprinkle lightly with paprika and enjoy.
Serves 2

Carbs per recipe: 23
Carbs per serving: 12

Scrambled Tofu

1 tablespoon coconut oil
1 tablespoon green onion, finely chopped
8 ounces firm tofu
8 ounces soft tofu
1/4 teaspoon curry powder
1/4 teaspoon cumin powder
1/4 teaspoon onion powder
1 tablespoon nutritional yeast*
Celtic salt and pepper to taste

Melt coconut oil in a skillet over medium-low heat. Add onion and sauté until it turns bright green. Meanwhile, crumble tofu into a bowl and mix with curry, cumin and onion powders. Add nutritional yeast. Add tofu mixture to skillet and sauté for 3 to 5 minutes or until done.
Serves 4

* Nutritional yeast is an excellent source of B vitamins and chromium.

Carbs per recipe: 12
Carbs per serving: 3

Tofu Mushroom Scramble

1 1/2 tablespoons coconut oil
1/2 pound mushrooms, sliced
1 pound firm tofu crumbled
1/4 teaspoon curry powder
1/4 teaspoon cumin powder
1/2 teaspoon onion powder
1 tablespoon nutritional yeast
2 tablespoons scallions, sliced
1/8 cup purified water
1/4 cup parsley, finely chopped
Celtic salt and pepper to taste

Melt one tablespoon coconut oil in a large skillet over medium-low heat. Add mushrooms and sauté until tender. While mushrooms are cooking, crumble tofu into a bowl and mix with curry, cumin and onion powders, and nutritional yeast. Transfer cooked mushrooms into a bowl and set aside. Melt remaining coconut oil in the skillet and pour in tofu mixture. Sauté for about two minutes. Add scallions, mushrooms and water, and cook for two more minutes, stirring constantly. Add chopped parsley, remove skillet from heat, cover with a lid and allow flavors to mingle for a few minutes before serving.
Serves 4

Carbs per recipe: 14
Carbs per serving: 4

Drinks

Sparkling Lemonade

1 fresh lemon, juiced
22 ounces of seltzer water
1/8 teaspoon stevia
12 ice cubes or as desired

Pour lemon juice, seltzer water and stevia into a pitcher and stir. Serve over ice, or as a variation, blend liquids with ice to make a refreshing slushy beverage.
Serves 4

Carbs per recipe: 6
Carbs per serving: 2

Cola "Float"

Ice cubes
1 ounce heavy cream
12-ounce can of a natural low-carb soda*

Pour a soda over ice cubes and cream for a frothy delicious drink. This can be served "on the rocks" or added to the blender as a cold slushy alternative.
Serves one

Carbs per recipe: 1
Carbs per serving: 1
(May vary based on product.)

* Natural product companies such as After the Fall now make herb-sweetened low-carb sodas. These are available in most health and natural food stores.

Creamy Flax Shake No. 1

8 ounces water
6 ice cubes
1/4 cup whey protein concentrate (vanilla or natural)
1/2 tablespoon flax oil
1 dash stevia

Add water, ice, whey protein and flax oil to blender. Blend until creamy adding stevia to taste and drink immediately.
Servings: 1

Carbs per recipe: 1
Carbs per serving: 1

Creamy Flax Shake No. 2

1 1/2 teaspoons flax seeds, soaked overnight
1 ounce purified water
8 ounces water
1/2 cup ice cubes
1 scoop whey protein concentrate (vanilla or natural)
1 dash stevia or to taste

Soak flax seeds in one ounce of water overnight. Add water, ice cubes, whey protein concentrate, flax seeds and soaking water to blender. Blend until thick and creamy. Servings: 1

Carbs per recipe: 4
Carbs per serving: 4

Superfood Smoothie

A great way to start the day, with excellent sources of protein, fiber, chlorophyll, essential fatty acids and more.

1 1/2 teaspoon flax seeds, soaked overnight
1 ounce purified water
1/8 cup vanilla flavored soy protein powder (low carb)
1/4 cup vanilla whey protein concentrate
1 tablespoon spirulina powder
12 ounces purified water
6 ice cubes

Soak flax seeds in one ounce of water overnight. Add seeds and soaking liquid, soy and whey protein powders, spirulina, water and ice into a blender. Blend on medium high until smooth.
Serves 1

Carbs per recipe: 6
Carbs per serving: 6

Strawberry Frappé

1/4 cup fresh cream
12 ounces seltzer water
1/2 cup ice
1/2 cup fresh or frozen strawberries (unsweetened)
2 dashes stevia extract powder

Add cream, mineral water, ice, strawberries and stevia to a blender. Blend on high speed until rich and frothy. Serve immediately.
Serves 2

Carbs per recipe: 8
Carbs per serving: 4

Raspberry Frappé

1 cup seltzer water
2 ounces cream
1 scoop vanilla whey protein
1/8 cup raspberries
1/2 cup ice
1 dash stevia rebaudiana

Add seltzer water, cream, whey protein, raspberries, ice and stevia into a blender.
Blend until smooth.
Serves 1

Carbs per recipe: 8
Carbs per serving: 8

Blueberry Smoothie

1 cup water
1/2 cup ice cubes
1/2 tablespoon flax oil
1/4 cup blueberries, fresh or frozen
1 scoop whey protein concentrate, vanilla or natural
1 tablespoon soy lecithin
1 dash stevia

Add water, ice cubes, flax oil, blueberries, soy lecithin and whey protein concentrate into blender. Blend until thick and creamy. Add pinch of stevia or to taste. Blend on pulse for 30 more seconds. Serve immediately.
Serves 1

Carbs per recipe: 8
Carbs per serving: 8

Hot Chocolate

1 cup cream
3 cups boiling water
4 tablespoons cocoa powder
1/4 teaspoon stevia extract
1 teaspoon vanilla

Warm cream in a two-quart pot on medium high until almost simmering. Stir in boiling water, cocoa powder, stevia and vanilla. Stir until thoroughly combined.
Serves 4

Carbs per recipe: 22
Carbs per serving: 6

Hot Ginger Toddy

3 cups boiling water
1 1-inch chunk fresh ginger, minced
1 generous pinch stevia extract
1 ounce cream

Pour hot water over minced ginger. Allow to steep for three minutes. Strain into two large mugs, add stevia and cream. Stir and enjoy.
Serves 2

Carbs per recipe: 3
Carbs per serving: 1 1/2

Iced Chocolate

4 tablespoons hot purified water
3 tablespoons cocoa powder
2 generous dashes stevia
1/2 teaspoon vanilla
2 cups purified cool water
3 tablespoons cream
6-8 ice cubes

Add hot water to cocoa powder and stevia and mash into a smooth paste. Stir in vanilla, cool water and cream. Pour mixture over ice and serve.
Serves 2

Carbs per recipe: 11
Carbs per serving: 6

Mocchacino

2 cup purified water
1 cup strong coffee (regular or decaf)
3 tablespoons cream
2/3 cup ice cubes
3 tablespoons cocoa powder
2 dashes stevia
1/3 cup whey protein concentrate, vanilla
1 tablespoon soy lecithin

Pour water, decaffeinated coffee, cream, ice cubes, cocoa, whey protein concentrate and lecithin into blender. Blend until rich and creamy. Add stevia to taste and blend on pulse for 30 seconds more.
Serves 2

Carbs per recipe: 14
Carbs per serving: 7

Appetizers

Savory Tofu Dip

**8 ounces firm tofu (try substituting cream cheese,
brie, sour cream or plain yogurt)**
1 tablespoon flax oil
1 tablespoon apple cider vinegar
2 tablespoons lemon juice
2 tablespoons green onion, finely chopped
1 tablespoon fresh dill, minced
1 teaspoon Bragg Aminos
8 ounces soft tofu

Place the firm tofu in a blender and add flax oil, apple cider vinegar, lemon juice, green onion, dill and Bragg Aminos. Blend until smooth and set aside. Mash soft tofu to the consistency of cottage cheese and add it to the blended mixture. Stir until thoroughly combined and refrigerate until ready to serve.
Makes 2 cups

Carbs per recipe: 15
Carbs 1 tablespoon: 8

Green Goddess Dip

1 large ripe avocado, peeled and chunked
6 ounces soft tofu, chunked
2 garlic cloves, chopped
3 tablespoons lemon juice
1 teaspoon tamari
1/8 teaspoon cayenne pepper

Add avocado chunks, tofu, garlic, lemon juice, tamari and cayenne pepper to a blender or food processor. Blend until creamy.
Makes about 1 cup

Carbs per recipe: 21
Carbs 1 tablespoon: 1

Party Veggie Dip

1 cup mayonnaise
1 cup sour cream
1 7-ounce can water chestnuts, drained and finely minced
1 tablespoon green onion, finely minced
2 tablespoons pimento, finely minced
2 teaspoons powdered chicken or vegetable broth
1/2 teaspoon Worcestershire sauce

In a medium-sized bowl, beat mayonnaise and sour cream until smooth. Add minced water chestnuts, onions and pimento. Add to the mix and stir. Sprinkle in the chicken broth and Worcestershire sauce and stir vigorously until well blended. Allow flavors to mingle by refrigerating at least three hours before serving.
Makes 2 1/2 cups

Carbs per recipe: 10
Carbs 1 tablespoon: 1/3

Mushroom Paté

*This recipe takes a little time, but it is absolutely delicious
and a "must-serve" for special guests.*

1/4 cup dried Shitake mushrooms
1 cup purified water
4 tablespoons butter
8 ounces fresh crimini mushrooms, sliced
1 leek, thinly sliced
2 tablespoons cognac
1/2 cup cream
2 anchovy fillets
4 tablespoons fresh parsley, chopped
2 garlic cloves
2 teaspoon shoyu or tamari sauce
1/8 teaspoon black pepper
2 tablespoons extra virgin olive oil
2 tablespoons butter, softened

Pour enough boiling purified water over the dried shitake mushrooms to cover; allow them to soak for about one hour. Drain mushrooms and set liquid aside. In a large skillet, heat butter over medium heat. Add shitake and crimini mushrooms and sauté them over medium heat until liquid is almost completely cooked off. Add sliced leek and sauté for one minute.

Continued on next page ...

Add cognac and cook until evaporated. Add the mushroom soaking liquid and cook until nearly dry. Add cream until nearly half-evaporated. Remove from heat and add mixture to a food processor. Add anchovies, parsley, garlic, tamari sauce and pepper. Process until mixture is finely chopped. Add butter and olive oil until thoroughly combined. Refrigerate at least three hours before serving.

Serve with fresh jicama slices or thin toasted wedges of soya bread (see section 9).
Makes about 1 1/2 cups

Carbs per recipe: 25
Carbs 1 tablespoon: 1

Eggplant Paté

1 large eggplant
1/4 cup onion, chopped
1 red pepper, cut into strips
2 tablespoons flax oil
1 tablespoon lemon juice
1 teaspoon balsamic vinegar
1 teaspoon fresh thyme
1/4 teaspoon fresh ground pepper

Bake whole, unpeeled eggplant in preheated oven at 350 for about 45 minutes or until skin is wrinkled and knife inserts easily. Remove from oven and allow to cool for about five minutes. Peel off the skin and chop eggplant into chunks. Place eggplant, onion and pepper strips into a food processor. Chop until fine and well mixed. Add oil, lemon juice, balsamic vinegar and spices. Chop until desired paté consistency. Serve with yellow, green and red pepper strips, jicama and celery.
Makes about 1 1/2 cups

Carbs per recipe: 43
Carbs 1 tablespoon: 2

Salmon Roll-Ups

8 thin slices smoked salmon (lox)
8 spears cooked asparagus (canned or steamed)
2 tablespoons mayonnaise
2 lemon wedges
2 parsley sprigs

Separate and flatten salmon slices on a large platter. Place an asparagus spear over each slice, smear with mayonnaise and wrap salmon around it. Garnish with lemon wedges and parsley sprigs. Double or triple recipe for dinner party or special occasion.
Serves 2

Carbs per recipe: 9
Carbs serving: 5

Thai Shrimp Cocktail

8 ounces large cooked prawns
1/2 cup cilantro, minced
2 tablespoons green chili dipping sauce (Thai Kitchen)
1 small lime, juiced
2 cups chopped lettuce
2 or 3 cilantro sprigs
Lime wedges

Place prawns in a medium-sized bowl. Add cilantro, green chili dipping sauce and lime juice. Stir ingredients until evenly combined. Place mixture over chopped lettuce and garnish with fresh cilantro sprigs and lime wedges.
Serves 2

Carbs per recipe: 10
Carbs serving: 5

Pickled Herring

2 large herring fillets (skinned and deboned)
1/2 medium yellow onion, thinly sliced
1/2 cup rice vinegar, unsweetened
2 tablespoons purified water
1/8 teaspoon stevia
1/4 teaspoon fresh ground pepper

Cut herring fillets into 1/2 inch strips and place, alternately with onion slices, in a medium-sized glass dish. Meanwhile, mix rice vinegar, water, stevia and ground pepper, and pour evenly over fish and onions. Cover and refrigerate for at least three hours.
Serves 8

Carbs per recipe: 16
Carbs serving: 2

Crab-Stuffed Cucumber

1 medium cucumber
1 teaspoon lemon juice
1/2 cup crab meat (real, not imitation)
2 tablespoons mayonnaise
1 ounce feta cheese, finely crumbled
Paprika, to taste

Peel cucumber and slice it in half lengthwise. Scoop out the seeds and drizzle both halves with lemon juice. In a small bowl, combine crab meat, mayonnaise and feta cheese until well blended. Stuff cucumber with crab mix, slice into bite-sized portions and sprinkle lightly with paprika.
Serves 4

Carbs per recipe: 8
Carbs per serving: 2

Deviled Eggs

8 eggs, hardboiled
1/2 cup celery, minced
2 tablespoons red onion, minced
4 tablespoons mayonnaise
1/2 teaspoon dry mustard
1/8 teaspoon salt
1/8 teaspoon pepper
16 black olive slices
Paprika

Cut eight hard-boiled eggs in half, lengthwise. Remove yolks and place in medium-sized bowl. Stir in celery, red onion, mayonnaise, dry mustard, salt and pepper. Spoon yolk mixture into whites and garnish black olive slices (one per egg half). Lightly dust eggs with paprika.
Serves 4

Carbs per recipe: 10
Carbs serving: 3

Baked Cabbage Roll-ups

3 cups cabbage, chopped
1/4 cup Swiss cheese, grated (1 ounce)
8 slices smoked turkey breast
2 tablespoons onion, chopped
1 tablespoon coconut oil
1 teaspoon flour
1/8 teaspoon pepper
1/3 cup cream
1/3 cup purified water
1 teaspoons horseradish
1/2 cup Swiss cheese
2 tablespoons parsley, chopped

Steam the cabbage for six minutes or until crispy tender. Place about 1/3 cup of the steamed cabbage and one tablespoon Swiss cheese on each turkey slice. Roll these up and place cabbage rolls in a shallow baking pan.

Melt coconut oil in a medium-sized saucepan. Add onion and cook until tender. Stir in flour and pepper. Add cream, water and horseradish. Cook and stir until thickened and bubbly. Stir in the remaining Swiss cheese and parsley until cheese is melted. Pour over cabbage rolls. Bake at 375 for about 15 minutes. Cool slightly, garnish with fresh minced parsley and serve.
Serves 4

Carbs per recipe: 24
Carbs per serving: 6

Easy Antipasto

1 medium-sized jar of artichoke hearts
1 6-ounce can salmon, drained
1 cup mixed pickled vegetables (remove carrots)
1 jar jalapeno-stuffed green olives
1 medium can black olives
4 ounces mozzarella cheese, chunked
8 ounces of tomato sauce
Fresh ground pepper to taste

Drain artichoke hearts and set liquid (marinade) aside. Place artichoke hearts, salmon, pickled vegetables, olives, and cheese in a medium sized bowl. Cover with tomato sauce and artichoke marinade. Toss mixture gently until evenly combined. Chill for several hours or overnight to allow flavors to blend. Sprinkle with fresh ground pepper to taste.
Serves 4

Carbs per recipe: 35
Carbs serving: 9

Snacks

Creamed Strawberries

1 cup cottage cheese
1/2 cup Designer® Protein (French vanilla)
3 tablespoons purified water
1/2 cup strawberries, sliced
a pinch of stevia extract powder
2 tablespoon slivered almonds

In a food processor, purée cottage cheese, whey protein concentrate, water, strawberries and stevia extract powder. Transfer into two bowls, sprinkle with slivered almonds and enjoy.
Serves 2

Carbs per recipe: 26
Carbs per serving: 13

Whey Healthy Protein Bars

1/4 cup almond butter
11/2 tablespoons purified water
11/2 tablespoons flax oil
2 pinches stevia
1 cup (3 scoops) Designer® Protein (French vanilla)

Combine almond butter, water, flax oil, stevia and whey protein concentrate until dry and crumbly. Transfer to waxed paper and continue blending by kneading mixture by hand until it has the consistency of bread dough. Either by hand or with a rolling pin, form dough into rectangular bars. Wrap in waxed paper and store in the refrigerator. Makes 4 bars

Carbs per recipe: 18
Carbs per bar: 5

Coconut Candy Balls

1/4 cup peanut butter
1/3 cup (1 scoop) Designer®
Protein (French vanilla)
1 teaspoon purified water or coconut milk
2 pinches stevia
1/2 teaspoon vanilla extract
1/4 cup unsweetened coconut, shredded

Place peanut butter, whey protein concentrate, vanilla, water or coconut milk, stevia, and two tablespoons of the shredded coconut by hand into a food processor and blend until thoroughly combined. Form mixture into 12 small balls and roll these in the remaining coconut. Keep these in the refrigerator.
Makes 12 candy balls

Carbs per recipe: 14
Carbs 1 tablespoon: 1

Almond Energy Balls

1/2 cup almonds
1 tablespoons purified water
1 tablespoons flax oil
2/3 cup (2 scoops) Designer® Protein
1/4 teaspoon almond extract
2 pinches stevia
2 tablespoons unsweetened coconut, shredded

Add almonds, water, oil, Designer Protein, almond extract and stevia to a food processor. Blend until smooth. Form 12 small balls, roll in coconut. Keep refrigerated.
Makes 12 balls

Total carbs: 33
Carbs per serving: 3

Sesame Bites

1 1/2 cups sesame seeds
1/3 cup coconut oil
2/3 cup Designer Protein
1/8 teaspoon stevia extract
1 teaspoon vanilla

Toast sesame seeds until golden brown. Grind 1/4 cup of the sesame seeds and set them aside. Place oil in food processor and blend on low while gradually adding the remaining sesame seeds and the Designer Protein. Add stevia and vanilla, and blend until smooth. Shape into 1/2-inch balls and roll them in the ground, toasted sesame seeds (optional: Add a tiny pinch of stevia to grounded sesame seeds).
Makes 16 "bites"

Carbs per recipe: 44
Carbs per serving: 3

Soups & Salads

Cucumber Basil Soup

6 cups purified water
3 English (seedless hot house)
cucumbers, peeled and sliced
1 small onion, chopped
1/8 teaspoon cayenne pepper
1 lemon, juiced
3 garlic cloves
3 medium sprigs basil, chopped
8 ounces sour cream

Pour water into a large pot. Add cucumber slices, onion, cayenne pepper, lemon juice, garlic and basil. Bring mixture to a boil, turn heat to medium-low and simmer for 15 minutes. Remove from heat and set aside until soup reaches room temperature. Transfer mixture into a blender or food processor and blend. Add sour cream and blend on low until smooth. Pour soup into a medium-sized serving bowl and refrigerate for at least three hours. Serve soup cold, garnished with finely chopped fresh basil.
Serves 4

Carbs per recipe: 56
Carbs per serving: 14

Garlic Gazpacho

4 fresh garlic cloves, minced
1 hot house cucumber, peeled and sliced
1 cup roma tomatoes, chopped
1 yellow bell pepper, chopped
1 cup fat-free chicken broth
4 ounces spicy tomato juice
1 tablespoon extra virgin olive oil
1 tablespoon Barlean's flax oil
1/4 cup fresh cilantro, finely chopped
1/2 teaspoon ground white pepper
2-3 small sprigs cilantro
2 tablespoons green onions, chopped

Wash and slice/chop cucumbers, tomatoes, garlic and bell pepper. Add chicken broth, spicy tomato juice, oils, cilantro and white pepper. Stir soup and top with extra cilantro and green onions for garnish. Chill for at least two hours before serving. Serves 4

Carbs per recipe: 32
Carbs per serving: 8

Cool Avocado Soup

2 ripe avocados, pitted and peeled
1 teaspoon lemon juice
1 1/2 cups cold chicken broth
1/2 cup cream
1/2 cup sour cream
1/2 cup chardonnay wine
2 tablespoons parsley, finely minced

Cut avocados into chunks and place in a blender or food processor. Add chicken broth, cream, sour cream, lemon and chardonnay. Blend until smooth. Serve cold, sprinkled with fresh finely minced parsley.
Serves 4

Carbs per recipe: 42
Carbs per serving: 11

Marinated Mushroom Soup

1 cup water
1/2 cup chardonnay
2 cups mushrooms, thinly sliced
1/4 cup onion, minced
1 bay leaf
1/2 teaspoon salt
1/4 teaspoon black pepper
1 pinch stevia
2 garlic cloves, minced
1 tablespoon fresh basil, minced
1 teaspoon fresh dill, minced
1/4 teaspoon dried thyme
2 tablespoons flax oil
2 tablespoons lemon juice
1 teaspoon cider vinegar
2 tablespoons chives, minced

Place water, chardonnay, mushrooms, onions, bay leaf, salt and pepper in a medium-sized pot over high heat. Bring to a boil, reduce heat to low, cover and allow soup to simmer for 15 minutes. Remove pot from the burner and add stevia, garlic, basil, dill, thyme, flax oil, lemon juice, cider vinegar and chives. Stir mixture and refrigerate for at least two hours. (tip: Do remove the bay leaf before serving).
Serves 4

Carbs per recipe: 45
Carbs per serving: 11

"Cream" of Spinach Soup

1 tablespoon coconut oil
1 small yellow onion, chopped
1 cup tomato juice
3 cups chicken broth
6 ounces firm tofu, cubed
1/2 pound spinach, washed and chopped
2 tablespoons minced fresh dill
1/8 teaspoon fresh ground black pepper
1/2 cup sour cream
3 garlic cloves, chopped

Heat coconut oil in a large pot, add chopped onion, and stir-fry until translucent. Add tomato juice, chicken broth, and tofu and simmer for 10 minutes. Next, add the spinach, dill and pepper, stirring over heat for one minute. Purée the soup in a blender with 1/4 cup sour cream and garlic (if necessary, blend in two batches to avoid over-filling blender). Reheat soup over medium heat before serving and garnish with remaining sour cream.
Serves 4

Carbs per recipe: 77
Carbs per serving: 19

Turkey Gumbo Stew

1 tablespoon coconut oil
1 medium onion, diced
1 green pepper, diced
1 cup celery, diced
8 cups turkey or chicken stock
4 cups turkey meat, chopped
3 tablespoons fresh parsley, finely chopped
2 teaspoons Bragg Liquid Aminos
2 garlic cloves, minced
2 teaspoons Creole seasoning
1 tablespoon file gumbo
2 cups okra, sliced

Melt coconut oil over medium heat and sauté onion, bell pepper and celery until tender. In a large pot over high heat, heat turkey or chicken stock to boiling and add sautéed vegetables and all remaining ingredients (except okra). Turn heat down to medium-low and simmer for 40 minutes. Add okra and simmer for 20 minutes. Season to taste and serve hot.
Serves 8

Carbs per recipe: 64
Carbs per serving: 8

Hot Tip: This soup grows more delicious over the following days. Try warming it up after a day or two for even more flavor.

Caribbean Vegetable Stew

1/4 cup onion, finely chopped
3 garlic cloves, minced
1 tablespoon coconut oil
1 tablespoon fresh ginger, finely minced
1 teaspoon turmeric powder
2 teaspoons coriander powder
1/2 teaspoon dried thyme
1/4 teaspoon allspice
4 cups water
4 cups kale, chopped
1 cup fresh okra, sliced
1 cup tomatoes, diced
2 tablespoons fresh lime juice
1 13-ounce can coconut milk

In a large soup pot, sauté onion and garlic in coconut oil over low heat for about five minutes. Add ginger, turmeric, coriander, thyme and allspice. Sauté for one more minute while stirring continuously. Add water and bring to a boil. Simmer for two minutes and stir in the kale. Add okra and simmer for an additional five minutes. Stir in tomatoes and lime juice and cook until all of the vegetables are tender.

Finally, stir in the coconut milk, and cook for just a few more minutes before serving. If desired, add more lime juice to taste.
Serves 4

Carbs per recipe: 66
Carbs per serving: 17

Fish Stew

1 tablespoon coconut oil
1 small onion, finely chopped
3 celery stalks, finely chopped
1 cup stewed tomatoes
1/2 cup white wine
1/4 teaspoon pepper
1/4 teaspoon cumin
1 cup clam juice
1 1/4 cup purified water
4 medium fish fillets (rainbow trout), sliced into bite-sized pieces
3 garlic cloves, finely minced
1/4 cup parsley, finely minced

Melt coconut oil in a large pot over medium heat. Add onion and celery and sauté until they are tender. Remove from heat. Place tomatoes, wine, pepper, cumin and clam juice in a blender and pulse-blend several times or until tomatoes are crushed. Add this mix plus water to the pot, turn heat to medium-high and simmer for about 15 minutes. Add fish and simmer for 10 more minutes.

Turn off heat and add garlic and parsley. Stir soup, cover pot and allow flavors to mingle for a few minutes before serving.
Serves 4

Carbs per recipe: 68
Carbs per serving: 17

Chinese Eggdrop Soup

1 tablespoon coconut oil
1 tablespoon toasted-sesame oil
1 inch ginger root, minced
1 cup green beans
1/2 cup mushrooms, thinly sliced
1/2 celery, thinly sliced
1 green onion (separate whites and greens)
1/4 cup low-sodium soy sauce
4 cups chicken stock
1 medium tomato, chopped
1 tablespoon rice vinegar
1 small pinch stevia
2 large eggs, beaten

Melt coconut oil over medium heat in a large pot. Add sesame oil, ginger root, green beans, mushrooms, celery and only the white portion of the onion slices. Stir-fry vegetables for four minutes. Add soy sauce, chicken stock and chopped tomato. Cover pot and cook for 10 more minutes. Turn heat to medium-high, add rice vinegar and stevia, allow soup to come to a gentle boil and gradually stir in beaten eggs. Cook for one more minute and serve hot, topped with fresh green onion slices.
Serves 4

Carbs per recipe: 24
Carbs per serving: 6

Tofu Okra Soup

1 tablespoon coconut oil
1 small onion, chopped
2 cups okra, stemmed and sliced
1 cup celery, diced
1 green pepper, chopped
1 large tomato, peeled and chopped
1/4 teaspoon Celtic salt
1/8 teaspoon pepper
1/8 teaspoon paprika
1 pinch stevia
2 1/2 cups boiling water
1 cup broiled tofu strips, chopped (see Main Dishes)

Melt coconut oil in a large pot over medium-high heat. Add onion, okra, celery and green pepper and sauté until vegetables are tender-crisp (about three minutes). Add chopped tomato, salt, pepper, paprika and stevia. Stir and gradually add boiling water. Cover pot and allow soup to simmer for 45 minutes. Add chopped tofu strips and simmer for 10 more minutes.
Serves 4

Carbs per recipe: 48
Carbs per serving: 12

Herbed Zucchini Soup

1 tablespoon coconut oil
1 small onion, chopped
2 cups zucchini, sliced
1/4 teaspoon thyme (dried)
1/4 teaspoon rosemary (dried)
1/4 teaspoon Celtic salt
1/8 teaspoon pepper
2 tablespoons fresh basil, minced
3 cups chicken broth
1/2 cup cream
2 sprigs fresh basil

Melt coconut oil in a large pot over medium heat. Sauté onion until tender. Add zucchini, thyme, minced basil, rosemary, salt and pepper. Stir-fry mixture for about five minutes. Add chicken broth, turn heat to medium-high and simmer for 15 minutes or until zucchini is tender. Transfer soup to blender and purée until smooth. Return soup to pot over medium heat and stir in cream. Cook for two more minutes, garnish with fresh basil leaves and serve hot.
Serves 4

Carbs per recipe: 32
Carbs per serving: 8

Chinese Cabbage Beef Soup

1/4 pound rump steak, sliced
2 teaspoons low-sodium soy sauce
1 tablespoon dry sherry
1 teaspoon toasted sesame oil
1 teaspoon coconut oil
3 cups purified water
2 cups Chinese cabbage, shredded
1 teaspoon soy sauce
1/4 teaspoon garlic powder

Slice steak into thin, bite-sized slices. Combine soy sauce, sherry and sesame oil, and drizzle over meat slices, allowing the meat to marinade for at least one hour. Melt coconut oil in a nonstick skillet over medium-high heat. Add meat and brown slightly. Remove from the skillet. In a medium-sized pot bring water to a boil. Add Chinese cabbage, beef, soy sauce and garlic powder. Cover, simmer for 10 minutes and serve. Serves 4

Carbs per recipe: 16
Carbs per serving: 4

Curried Chicken Soup

1 tablespoon coconut oil
1/2 tablespoon arrow root
1 tablespoon curry powder
3 cups chicken broth
1/4 teaspoon paprika
1/2 teaspoon Celtic salt
1 egg yolk
1/4 cup cream
1 cup chicken meat, cooked and chopped
2 tablespoons parsley, minced

Melt coconut oil in a medium-sized pot over low heat. Stir in arrow root and curry powder. Increase heat to medium-high. Slowly stir in chicken broth and allow to cook until boiling. Add paprika and salt. Reduce heat to low.

Whisk egg yolk with cream and stir into soup until slightly thickened. Add chicken meat and cook for 3 more minutes. Garnish with minced parsley and serve.
Serves 4

Carbs per recipe: 8
Carbs per serving: 2

High Energy Vegetable Salad

4 cups baby salad mix
1/2 ripe avocado, sliced
1/2 cup fresh mushrooms, sliced
1/2 cup red cabbage, chopped
1 celery stalk, finely chopped
4 large radishes, sliced
1 cup alfalfa sprouts
2 tablespoons cilantro, minced

Fill a large salad bowl with baby salad mix, avocado, mushrooms, red cabbage and celery. Toss vegetables lightly, and top with radishes, sprouts and cilantro as salad garnish. Serve with favorite low-carb dressing.
Serves 2

Carbs per recipe: 20
Carbs per serving: 10

Napa Cabbage Slaw

1 large head Napa cabbage, finely chopped
1 red bell pepper, seeded and sliced
1 small hot house cucumber, trimmed, halved and sliced
1 green onion, finely chopped
2 tablespoons sesame seeds, toasted

Place all ingredients except sesame seeds into a large bowl. Add **Chinese Salad Dressing** (See Dressings, Spreads & Sauces), toss lightly, making sure to combine mixture thoroughly. Refrigerate for one hour. Garnish with toasted sesame seeds.
Serves 4

Carbs per recipe: 37
Carbs per serving: 9

Simple Coleslaw

1/3 cup mayonnaise
1 pinch stevia
1 small head of green cabbage, finely chopped
1/2 cup red cabbage, finely chopped

In a medium-sized bowl, stir stevia into mayonnaise. Add chopped green and red cabbage and thoroughly combine. Chill coleslaw for at least one hour and stir gently before serving.
Serves 6

Carbs per recipe: 22
Carbs per serving: 4

Creamy Broccoli Salad

1 pound fresh broccoli
1/4 cup mayonnaise
1/4 cup sour cream
3 tablespoons fresh lemon juice
1/4 teaspoon dried tarragon, crushed
1 scallion, finely minced
1/4 teaspoon pepper

Steam broccoli (trimmed stalks and florets) until tender-crisp. Rinse with cold water and drain. Place mayonnaise, sour cream, lemon juice, tarragon, scallion and pepper in a medium sized bowl and stir until smooth. Add broccoli and toss salad until evenly combined.
Serves 6

Carbs per recipe: 44
Carbs per serving: 7

Steamed Vegetable Salad

1 cup broccoli florets
1 cup cauliflower, cut
1 cup summer squash, sliced
2 cups baby salad mix
2 tablespoons basil, chopped
1/4 cup sunflower seed sprouts
1 tablespoon sunflower seeds, toasted
1 ounce farmer's cheese, grated (optional)

Steam broccoli florets, cauliflower and summer squash until lightly tender. Set aside to cool. Place baby salad mix and chopped basil in a medium-sized serving bowl and use finger tips to gently mix. Toast sunflower seeds until golden brown. Pour (warm) vegetables over lettuce and basil. Top with sunflower seed sprouts, salad dressing and sunflower seeds. If extra protein or flavor is desired, add grated farmer's cheese. Serves 2

Carbs per recipe: 19
Carbs per serving: 10

California Health Salad

2 cups Boston lettuce
2-inch piece hothouse cucumber, sliced
1/2 small tomato, sliced
1 tablespoon green sliced onion
1/8 avocado, sliced
2 radishes, sliced
1/2 cup alfalfa sprouts
1/4 cup sunflower sprouts

Wash and shred lettuce and place it in a serving bowl. Slice cucumber, tomato, onion, avocado and radishes and place it over the lettuce. Top salad with alfalfa, sunflower sprouts and favorite low carb dressing.
1 serving

Carbs per recipe: 10
Carbs per serving: 2

Tofu "Egg" Salad

1 pound firm tofu (or substitute hard boil eggs)
2 tablespoons minced green onion
1/2 cup celery, finely minced
2 teaspoons prepared mustard
1 pinch turmeric
1/8 teaspoon ground pepper
1/3 cup mayonnaise

Mash tofu to the consistency of finely chopped eggs. Add onion, celery, mustard, turmeric, pepper and mayonnaise. Thoroughly combine this mixture until it resembles egg salad. Serve over a bed of lettuce for a delicious vegetarian meal.
Serves 4

Carbs per recipe: 11
Carbs per serving: 3

Salmon Salad

1 pound cooked salmon, flaked
1/2 cup celery, minced
1 tablespoon onion, minced
1 tablespoon pimento, minced
1 tablespoon parsley
2 tablespoons fresh lemon juice
1/4 cup mayonnaise
4 large lettuce leaves

Combine flaked salmon, celery, parsley, onion and pimento in a medium-sized bowl. Drizzle with lemon juice and use a fork to mix in the mayonnaise. Spoon onto a plate covered with four large lettuce leaves — or serve with the California Salad for extra protein.
Serves 4

Carbs per recipe: 4
Carbs per serving: 1

Taco Salad

4 cups of Romaine lettuce, chopped
8 ounces ground beef
2 tablespoons taco seasoning (no sugar)
1 green onion, finely chopped
1/4 cup tomato, chopped
1/6 avocado, chopped
4 black olives, sliced
2 ounces cheddar cheese, grated
2 tablespoons sour cream

Arrange two or three large, whole Romaine lettuce leaves on a large plate. Brown ground beef in a medium skillet and mix in taco seasoning. Divide chopped lettuce equally between the two plates. Top with beef, onion, tomatoes, avocado, olives and grated cheese. Garnish with sour cream.
Serves 2

Carbs per recipe: 20
Carbs per serving: 10

Chef's Salad

1 1/2 cups Romaine lettuce, rinsed
and julienned
1 1/2 cups red leaf lettuce, rinsed and
julienned
1 cup raw, chopped low carb vegetables (mix and match):
    broccoli, celery, cucumber, jicama, onions, peppers, radishes,
    mushrooms
4 ounces turkey breast (fresh, not processed), cut in strips
1 hard-boiled egg, sliced
1 ounce Swiss cheese, cut in strips
1 ounce cheddar cheese, cut in strips
1 ounce alfalfa sprouts

Place lettuce in a large salad bowl and toss with chopped, mixed vegetables. Arrange turkey meat, egg slices and cheese on top of the salad. Garnish with alfalfa sprouts and serve with any low carb dressing.
Serves 2

Carbs per recipe: 14
Carbs per serving: 7

Spinach Basil Salad

4 cups fresh baby spinach, washed and drained
2 sprigs basil, minced
1 tablespoon green onion, thinly sliced
2 tablespoons flax or olive oil
1 tablespoons lemon juice
1 teaspoon Bragg Liquid Aminos

Wash and drain spinach. Place in a medium bowl. Add basil and green onion. Drizzle with lemon juice, flax or olive oil and Bragg Liquid Aminos. Toss and enjoy.
Serves 2

Carbs per recipe: 10
Carbs per serving: 5

Avocado Shrimp Boats

4 cups baby lettuce
1 cup alfalfa sprouts
1 avocado, halved and peeled
1 cup shrimp, cooked, peeled and deveined
1 green onion, sliced
Lemon slices

Place two cups of baby lettuce in two salad bowls. Divide sprouts into two servings and arrange over lettuce. Place one avocado half over sprouts and fill each with 1/2 cup shrimp. Sprinkle onions over shrimp boats and garnish with lemon slices.
Serves 2

Carbs per recipe: 16
Carbs per serving: 8

Dressings, Spreads & Sauces

Tofu Herb Dressing

8 ounces soft tofu
1/4 cup rice vinegar (unsweetened
1 tablespoon low-sodium soy sauce
2 tablespoons flax oil
2 tablespoons red pepper, finely minced
2 tablespoons fresh parsley, finely minced
1 teaspoon fresh dill, minced
2 garlic cloves, finely minced
1/4 teaspoon black pepper

Place tofu, vinegar and soy sauce in a blender or food processor and puree until smooth. Add flax oil, red pepper, parsley, dill, garlic and pepper and blend for one more minute.

Makes about 2 1/3 cups

Carbs per recipe: 15

Lemon Olive Dressing

1/4 cup extra virgin olive oil
1/4 cup fresh flax oil
3 tablespoons lemon juice, fresh
1 tablespoon Bragg Liquid Aminos

Whisk olive oil, flax oil, lemon juice and Bragg Aminos until thoroughly combined. Use this dressing right away and store any remaining dressing in a sealed container in the refrigerator. Be sure to use within a few days.
Makes 3/4 cup

Carbs per recipe: 4

Lime-Basil Dressing

1/4 cup extra virgin olive oil
1/4 cup fresh flax oil
3 tablespoons lime juice, fresh
1/4 cup fresh basil
2 teaspoons Bragg Liquid Aminos

Combine olive oil, flax oil, lime juice, basil and Bragg Aminos in a food processor until smooth. Use right away and keep remaining dressing in a sealed container in the refrigerator. Use it up within a few days.
Makes about 3/4 cup

Carbs per recipe: 5

Mia's Favorite Dressing

(I make this in small quantities and use it up within a day or two.)

1/4 cup flax seed oil
1/8 cup extra virgin olive oil
2 teaspoons Bragg Liquid Aminos
1 tablespoon fresh lemon juice
1 fresh garlic clove, minced

Pour ingredients into a salad dressing bottle. Shake well and refrigerate overnight to allow flavors to mingle. Use within a two or three days.
Makes 1/2 cup

Carbs per recipe: 5

Fresh Garlic-Rosemary Dressing

1/3 cup extra virgin olive oil
1/3 cup flax seed oil
1/4 cup fresh rosemary, with stems removed
Juice of one lemon
3 tablespoons low-sodium soy sauce
3 tablespoon balsamic vinegar
1/2 teaspoon lemon zest (finely grated lemon rind)
3 garlic cloves

Add oils, rosemary, lemon juice, soy sauce, vine-gar, lemon zest and garlic cloves to a blender or food processor and blend until smooth. Refrigerate for at least 12 hours to allow flavors to mingle. Shake well before serving over fresh green salad or steamed vegetables.
Makes about 1 cup

Carbs per recipe: 17

Chinese Salad Dressing

(Great over Napa Cabbage Slaw)

1/4 cup rice vinegar (unsweetened)
3 tablespoons soy sauce
1 pinch stevia extract
1 tablespoon toasted sesame seed oil
1 teaspoon Thai Kitchen red chili paste

Place all ingredients in a medium bowl and whisk until thoroughly combined. Refrigerate until ready to use. Then rewhisk before adding to salad or slaw.
Makes 1/2 cup

Carbs per recipe: 6

Creamy Blue Cheese Dressing

4 ounces blue or Roquefort cheese, crumbled
1/2 cup mayonnaise
1/2 cup sour cream
1 teaspoon lemon juice
1 pinch stevia
1/2 teaspoon garlic powder

Place blue cheese, mayonnaise, sour cream, lemon juice, stevia and garlic powder into blender and pulse blend two or three times. The blue cheese should be partially blended with small chunks of blue cheese remaining for texture. Keeps fresh in refrigerator for about one week.
Makes 1 1/2 cups

Carbs per recipe: 11

Green Goddess Dressing

(Great with seafood salads!)

1/2 cup mayonnaise
1/2 cup sour cream
1/2 cup soft tofu
4 garlic cloves, chopped
1/3 cup fresh parsley, chopped
3 tablespoons chives, chopped
1 tablespoon lemon juice
1 tablespoon tarragon vinegar
2 tablespoons cream
1/2 teaspoon Celtic sea salt
1/2 teaspoon black pepper

Add mayonnaise, sour cream, tofu, parsley, chives, garlic, lemon juice, vinegar, cream, salt and pepper to a blender or food processor. Blend until green and smooth. Makes about 2 cups

Carbs per recipe: 23

Tofu-Mayo

1 pound soft tofu, washed and drained
1/4 cup lecithin granules
2 tablespoons lemon juice
2 tablespoons apple cider vinegar
1 teaspoon Bragg Amino Acids
1 tiny pinch stevia (optional)
3/4 cup flax oil

Cut tofu in one-inch chunks and place them into a food processor or blender. Add lecithin granules, lemon juice, apple cider vinegar, Bragg Amino Acids, stevia extract and 1/3 cup of oil. Blend on medium-high speed until thoroughly mixed. Very slowly and gradually add remaining oil. Blend for about three minutes or until very thick and creamy. Chill and use it up within a week.
Makes 2 cups

Carbs per recipe: 10

Tip: *If you use any of these mayonnaise recipes for making coleslaw, add a pinch of stevia for sweetness.*

Flax-Olive Mayonnaise

1 large egg
2 tablespoons cider vinegar
2 tablespoons lemon juice
1/2 teaspoon dry mustard
1 pinch salt
3/4 cup olive oil
1/2 cup flax oil

Place egg, vinegar, mustard and salt in a blender. Blend mixture on low. Combine olive and flax oils in an easy-pour measuring cup and slowly add oil mixture to blender in a thin stream (keep the blender on low). Add the lemon juice, and slowly add the remaining olive oil.
Makes 1 1/2 cups

Carbs per recipe: 5

Flax-Nut Mayonnaise

(This makes an excellent salad dressing base.)

1/2 cup raw almonds
1/4 cup purified water
1/3 cup flax oil
1 tablespoon nutritional yeast
2 tablespoons lemon juice
1/4 teaspoon garlic powder (optional)
1/4 teaspoon sea salt

Tip: For variation, add one teaspoon fresh minced dill

Soak almonds in water overnight. Drain the almonds and place them in a food processor or blender. Add flax oil, nutritional yeast, lemon juice, garlic powder and sea salt. Blend on high speed until thick and creamy. Refrigerate immediately. Keeps fresh for about one week.
Makes about 3/4 cup

Carbs per recipe: 24

Flax-Coconut "Butter"

Use this healthy spread in place of margarine or butter. It is a rich source of EFAs and MCTs.

8 ounces coconut oil
3 1/2 ounces flax oil
Celtic sea salt — to taste

Melt coconut oil. Remove flax oil from the freezer and add it to coconut oil, stirring until thoroughly blended. Add salt to taste. For a harder product, use more coconut oil.

Makes about 3/4 cup

Carbs per recipe: 0

Tip: *For variety, add minced garlic, green pepper or onion*

Avocado Spread

1 medium avocado
2 tablespoons Designer® Protein (natural)
1 teaspoon lemon juice
4 garlic cloves, finely minced
1/4 red pepper, finely minced
2 tablespoons cilantro, minced
3-4 dashes Tabasco sauce

Mash avocado to desired consistency and combine with whey protein concentrate and lemon juice. Mix in garlic, red pepper, tomato and cilantro. Drizzle lightly with Tabasco sauce and serve with seafood, on Soya bread (see Baking) or fresh vegetable slices.

Carbs per recipe: 24

Dill Sauce

(A delicious complement to Salmon Mousse. See Main Dishes.)

2/3 cup sour cream
1/4 cup mayonnaise
1/2 teaspoon Dijon mustard
2 tablespoon fresh dill, minced

Place sour cream, mayonnaise, mustard and dill in a small bowl and combine with a fork or spoon. For best taste, refrigerate for several hours. If serving with Salmon Mousse, spread sauce over a large serving platter and invert Mousse directly over the sauce.

Makes about 1 cup

Carbs per recipe: 21

Hollandaise Sauce

Great over asparagus, poached eggs and spinach —
or as a dipping sauce for Steamed Artichokes (see Vegetables)

1/2 cup butter
4 egg yolks, beaten
2 1/2 tablespoons lemon juice
pinch salt
pinch white pepper
pinch paprika (optional)

Melt two tablespoons of the butter over a double boiler. Beat egg yolks in a small bowl and gradually add melted butter to the yolks, whisking constantly. Pour the mixture back into the double boiler and replace it over the hot water. Add remaining butter by the teaspoon, while continuing to stir. When butter is completely melted, remove sauce from heat and stir in lemon juice, salt, pepper and paprika.
Makes about 1 cup

Carbs per recipe: 9

Lively Garlic Sauce

1/2 cup olive oil
1/2 cup flax oil
4 garlic cloves, pressed
1 large egg
1 egg yolk
1/2 teaspoon Celtic salt

Combine olive and flax oils in an easy-pour container. Place garlic, egg, egg yolk, salt and 1/4 cup of the oil into a blender and blend on low for about five seconds. Continue blending while slowly adding oil combination, as with mayonnaise. This thick, fragrant sauce is best served over steamed vegetables or with light meats. Use within three to four days.
Makes about 1 1/4 cups

Carbs per recipe: 4

Italian Pesto

1 large bunch basil, finely chopped
4 garlic cloves, chopped
1/4 cup pine nuts
1/4 cup Parmesan cheese
1/4 cup olive oil
1/8 cup flax oil

Place basil, garlic, pine nuts and Parmesan cheese in a blender or food processor. Blend until thoroughly chopped and mixed. Continue processing while gradually adding olive and flax oils. Blend until smooth. Use within two days.
Makes about 1 cup

Carbs per recipe: 12

Creamy Pesto: add one ounce cream cheese to Italian Pesto; blend until smooth. Use as a condiment with broiled chicken or fish.

Zesty Cucumber Sauce

1 cup cucumber, peeled and grated
1 cup mayonnaise
3 tablespoons lemon juice
1/4 teaspoon lemon zest
4 garlic cloves, pressed
1/2 teaspoon prepared mustard
Fresh ground pepper, to taste

Place cucumber, mayonnaise, lemon juice, lemon zest, garlic cloves, mustard and pepper in a bowl and stir until evenly combined. Delicious over fish salad or fish mousse. Can also be used as a salad dressing
Makes about 2 1/4 cups

Carbs per recipe: 11

Teriyaki Marinade

1/3 cup low-sodium soy sauce
2 tablespoons purified water
2 teaspoons rice vinegar (unsweetened)
1 teaspoon powdered ginger
1/4 teaspoon stevia

Combine soy sauce, water, rice vinegar, ginger and stevia. Use this sauce to marinate tofu, chicken, beef or pork before grilling or stir-frying. Modify this recipe quantity, depending on the amount of food being marinated. Remaining sauce can also be used for stir-fry.
Makes about 1/2 cup

Carbs per recipe: 11

Lemon Garlic Dunking Butter

*Perfect for dipping lobster, crab or artichoke
leaves. Also very good over steamed green beans or
asparagus. The addition of flax oil provides essential fatty acids,
and the taste blends in beautifully. Be sure to add the oil after butter is
removed from heat.*

**1/2 cup butter
2 tablespoon lemon juice
2 garlic cloves, pressed
1/8 cup flax oil**

Melt butter in a small saucepan over low heat. Remove from heat, stir in lemon juice,
garlic and flax oil, and serve.
Makes about 3/4 cup

Carbs per recipe: 5

Cool Curry Sauce

1 cup sour cream
1/8 cup green onion, finely minced
2 teaspoons curry powder
1 tiny pinch stevia

Place sour cream, green onion, curry powder and stevia into a small bowl. Stir until smooth and evenly combined. Serve with grilled lamb, chicken or pork.

Tip: best with curry- or Indian-seasoned meats or vegetables
Makes about 1 cup

Carbs per recipe: 19

Main Dishes

Peppered Szechwan

1 pound meat of choice or firm tofu, cut into bite-sized chunks
2 tablespoons coconut oil
1 green pepper, cut into thin strips
1 red pepper, cut into thin strips
1 yellow pepper, cut into thin strips
1/4 cup scallions, thinly sliced
1 tablespoon coconut oil
1/4 cup dry white wine
2 1/2 tablespoons soy sauce
1/2 cup water
1 teaspoon dry mustard
1/2 teaspoon dry hot pepper, crushed
3 garlic cloves, minced

Heat two tablespoons coconut oil in a large skillet over medium heat. Fry the tofu chunks until they turn a light golden brown. Drain them with a paper towel, place them on a baking sheet and keep them in the oven on low. Melt one tablespoon coconut oil in the skillet and begin to stir-fry red, green and yellow pepper strips and scallions over medium heat (about three minutes).

Combine and whisk white wine, soy sauce, water, mustard, garlic and hot pepper. Pour the liquid over the peppers and continue to stir-fry for eight more minutes. Add the meat or tofu and garlic, stir, cover and serve within minutes.
Serves 4

Carbs per recipe: 65
Carbs per serving: 16

Broiled Tofu Strips

This vegan entree can be served as a main dish, substituted for meat in many recipes or eaten as a cold snack.

1 pound extra-firm tofu

Marinade:
4 tablespoons low-sodium soy sauce
1 tablespoon extra virgin olive oil
1 tablespoon lemon juice
1 teaspoon Dijon mustard
1/2 teaspoon garlic powder
1 pinch stevia

Cut tofu into 1/2-inch-by-2-inch strips and arrange them evenly in a shallow baking pan. Whisk soy sauce, olive oil, lemon juice, mustard, garlic powder and stevia and pour over tofu strips. Marinate over a one- to two-hour period. Remove tofu strips and broil for about five minutes on each side or until lightly browned.
Serves 4

Carbs per recipe: 22
Carbs per serving: 6

Vegetarian "Cheese"

This soy-based treat can be substituted for cheese in a variety of recipes or served on a "cheese platter" for a light meal or snack.

1 cup white miso
1 pound block of extra-firm tofu

Rinse tofu under cool water and place it on a plate covered with 1/4 inch of miso. Cover remaining tofu with remaining miso. Wrap with a cheesecloth and place in a cool area, such as inside a dark cupboard. The tofu will ferment over one to two days, depending on desired taste. As it does so, it will emit a light beer-like aroma, which indicates that the fermentation is taking place. When the "cheese" is ready, remove the miso and rinse tofu under cool water.
Serves 4

Carbs per recipe: 21 (after miso has been removed)
Carbs per serving: 5

Herbal Goat Cheese Souffle

8 large eggs, separated
1/2 teaspoon cream of tartar
1/4 teaspoon Celtic sea salt
4 ounces crumbled chevre
(goat cheese)
1/4 cup fresh basil, finely
chopped
2 tablespoon chives, finely chopped
2 tablespoons butter or coconut oil

Separate the eggs. Beat whites on high speed with 1/2 teaspoon cream of tartar and 1/4 teaspoon salt until stiff. In a small bowl, beat egg yolks for two minutes until thick. Stir yolks while gradually adding crumbled chevre, basil and chives. Fold mixture into egg whites until evenly combined.

Melt butter or coconut oil over medium heat. Add the egg mixture and cook omelette-style for three minutes. Remove skillet from the stove, transfer to the oven and bake at 375 for 20 minutes or until golden brown.
Serves 4

Carbs per recipe: 4
Carbs per serving: 1

Creamy Broccoli Custard

6 cups broccoli florets
2 tablespoons butter
1 tablespoon cornstarch
1 cup cream
2/3 cup water
1/4 teaspoon Celtic salt
1/4 teaspoon pepper
1/8 teaspoon nutmeg
4 eggs

Steam broccoli florets until tender. Place them in a food processor, puree and set them aside. Melt the butter in a medium-sized saucepan over medium heat. Combine cream with water. Gradually add cornstarch, cream-water combination, salt, pepper and nutmeg (in this order) to the melted butter, while continuously mixing with a whisk. Once sauce begins to boil, reduce heat to low and continue simmering until it thickens. Remove from heat.

Preheat oven at 350. In a medium-sized bowl, thoroughly beat eggs, add puréed broccoli and cream sauce. Mix ingredients and pour into a casserole dish. Place dish in a metal baking pan and add water halfway up the side of the casserole dish. Bake for 45 minutes or until inserted toothpick comes out clean. Serve within five minutes. Serves 6

Carbs per recipe: 60
Carbs per serving: 10

Asparagus Frittata

1 pound asparagus
12 eggs
1/3 cup Parmesan cheese
1/3 cup cheddar cheese
1/4 teaspoon Celtic sea salt
1/4 teaspoon fresh ground pepper
1/2 teaspoon garlic powder
1 tablespoons coconut oil

Cut the asparagus into bite-sized pieces and steam until tender. Beat eggs and stir in asparagus, Parmesan cheese, cheddar cheese, salt, pepper and garlic powder. Melt coconut oil in a large skillet and cook over medium heat. Add egg mixture and cook for about 15 minutes, occasionally lifting frittata at the edges to let the uncooked eggs to flow underneath. For a golden top, remove from stove top, top with Parmesan cheese, and broil in the oven for about two minutes.
Serves 6

Carbs per recipe: 10
Carbs per serving: 1

Delicious Crab Scramble

*This makes a delicious main dish,
and can also be eaten cold as a snack.*

**4 eggs
2 tablespoons cream
4 ounces cooked crab meat, flaked
1 tablespoon coconut oil
1/4 cup leek, chopped
1 teaspoon Bragg Liquid Aminos
2 tablespoons Parmesan cheese, grated
1 tablespoon parsley, finely shopped**

Thoroughly beat eggs with cream. Mix in flaked crab meat. Melt coconut oil over medium heat, sauté chopped leek until tender. Add Bragg Liquid Aminos followed by egg mixture. Scramble until eggs are cooked. Transfer to plates, sprinkle with Parmesan cheese and parsley.
Serves 2

Carbs per recipe: 5
Carbs per serving: 3

Zucchini Casserole

1 pound small zucchini, sliced
1/4 cup onion, finely chopped
2 tablespoons butter
4 eggs
1 cup cream
1/2 teaspoon Celtic salt
1/8 teaspoon pepper
1/2 cup shredded sharp Cheddar cheese

Steam sliced zucchini until lightly tender and set aside. Sauté chopped onion in butter until tender. Beat eggs with cream, salt and pepper. Place zucchini into a buttered one-quart casserole dish, top with onions and with egg mixture. Sprinkle with grated cheese and bake in a preheated oven at 350 for 45 minutes or until inserted toothpick comes out clean.
Serve 4

Carbs per recipe: 85
Carbs per serving: 21

Sautéed Sole with Garlic

1 tablespoon coconut oil
1 pound sole (4 fillets)
3 cloves garlic
3 tablespoons fresh lemon juice
2 tablespoons parsley

Melt coconut oil in skillet over medium-high heat. Add sole and sauté for about five minutes, turning just once. Turn the heat off and remove skillet from stove. Top with chopped garlic, lemon juice and parsley and allow it to sit for at least one minute before serving.
Serves 2

Carbs per recipe: 7
Carbs per serving: 4

Halibut Fiesta Stirfry

1 pound fresh halibut steaks
1/4 cup fresh cilantro, minced
2 tablespoons chili seasoning (unsweetened)
2 tablespoons lime juice
2 garlic cloves, minced
2 tablespoons coconut oil
1 tablespoon onion, finely chopped
1/2 red pepper cut into 1/8-inch thin strips
1/2 green pepper cut into 1/8-inch thin strips

Cut halibut into bite-sized (about half inch) cubes and place into a medium-sized bowl. Add cilantro, chili seasoning, lime juice and garlic. Mix thoroughly. Cover fish and place it in the refrigerator to marinate for at least 30 minutes. When ready, heat a 10-inch skillet over medium heat. Melt coconut oil and add onions and peppers.

Sauté for about three minutes or until lightly tender. Remove vegetables and add fish mixture to the skillet. Cook for about four minutes or until fish lightly flakes. Return vegetables to the skillet and heat entire mixture for another minute or two. Garnish with fresh cilantro and sour cream, and serve with a finger-plate of fresh cucumber slices and salsa.
Serves 2

Carbs per recipe: 30
Carbs per serving: 15

Salmon Mousse

1 pound fresh salmon, cooked and cooled
or 1 large can (15 1/2 ounce) salmon
1/8 cup onion, sliced
1 large lemon, juiced
1 envelope unflavored
gelatin
1/3 cup boiling water
1/2 cup sour cream
1/2 cup mayonnaise
1 teaspoon paprika
1/3 cup fresh dill

Thoroughly coat a one-quart fish-shaped mold the liquid (water and oil) of the steamed or canned salmon. Discard remaining liquid. Put onion slices and lemon juice into a blender or food processor. Sprinkle gelatin over them and pour about half of the boiling water over them. Puree the mixture on low speed, while gradually adding the remainder of the boiling water.

Add sour cream, mayonnaise, paprika and dill until well blended. Stop the blender and add the salmon (in small chunks). Purée for another minute or two, until ingredients are thoroughly combined. Pour mixture into the mold and refrigerate for at least three hours, or until firm. To remove mousse from mold, insert a thin-bladed knife just under the mold and run the tip of the knife around the entire mold. Invert mousse onto a platter. For a special treat, serve with Dill Sauce (see Sauces)
Serves 4

Carbs per recipe: 20
Carbs per serving: 5

Garlic and Peppers Shrimp

1 green pepper
1 yellow pepper
1 red pepper
2 tablespoons butter
20 large deveined shrimp
2 teaspoons red chili paste
2 teaspoons lemon juice
4 garlic cloves, minced

Cut green, yellow and red peppers into 1/2-inch strips. Melt butter in a large skillet on medium-high heat and sauté the peppers for one minute. Add shrimp and stir fry until they turn bright pink. Season with chili paste and lemon juice, gently stirring over heat for on or two more minutes. Add garlic, remove from heat, cover skillet and allow flavors to mingle for a few more minutes or until dish is served.
Serves 4

Carbs per recipe: 58
Carbs per serving: 15

Oven-Broiled Crab Cakes

1 pound crab meat (lumped, not flaked)
1 tablespoon parsley, minced
1 tablespoon red pepper, minced
1 teaspoon lemon juice
1 teaspoon dry mustard
1/2 teaspoon garlic powder
1/2 teaspoon Celtic salt
2 eggs, beaten
1 teaspoon butter
Fresh lemon, sliced

Place crab meat in a medium bowl. Add parsley, red pepper, lemon juice, dry mustard, garlic powder, salt and beaten eggs. Gently stir mixture until evenly combined.

Butter a flat broiling pan. Form into 3-inch cakes, place evenly onto pan, and broil for four minutes or until golden brown. Turn crab cakes once and serve hot, garnished with fresh lemon slices.
Serves 4

Carbs per recipe: 5
Carbs per serving: 1

Zesty Salmon

2 salmon fillets, 6 ounces each
1 tablespoon butter
1/4 cup chicken broth
1 tablespoon lemon juice
1/2 teaspoon lemon zest, finely grated
2 garlic cloves, finely minced
pepper and paprika to taste
parsley sprigs.

Heat a large nonstick skillet over medium heat. Melt butter in skillet and add salmon fillets. Cook salmon for about five minutes on each side or until fish flakes lightly when tested with a fork. Transfer salmon to platter and place in warm oven. Meanwhile, keep skillet over medium heat and add chicken broth, lemon juice, lemon zest and garlic. Stir and cook mixture for about two minutes, pour over fresh cooked salmon and serve. Sprinkle with pepper and paprika to taste and serve garnished with parsley sprigs.
Serves 2

Carbs per recipe: 3
Carbs per serving: 2

Chicken Asparagus

1 tablespoon coconut oil
2 tablespoons onion, chopped
1 cup sliced mushrooms
1 pound skinless, boneless chicken breasts, cut into bite-sized strips
1 teaspoon lemon zest
2 tablespoons lemon juice
3/4 cup chicken broth
3 cups asparagus tips
3 garlic cloves, minced
2 tablespoons fresh parsley, minced
Fresh ground pepper

Sauté onion in coconut oil for about one minute. Add mushrooms and asparagus tips and sauté for two more minutes. Transfer to a bowl and set aside. Add chicken to the pan and sauté until lightly browned (about three minutes). Return the vegetables, along with the lemon zest, juice and chicken broth. Stir mixture, allowing it to simmer for about 10 minutes. Add garlic and parsley, cover with lid and remove from heat. Allow flavors to mingle for a few minutes and serve lightly sprinkled with ground pepper.
Serves 4

Carbs per recipe: 20
Carbs per serving: 5

Chicken Curry

2 tablespoons coconut oil
1/4 cup onion, chopped
1 tablespoon fresh ginger, minced
3 garlic cloves, minced
1 1/2 tablespoons curry powder
1 teaspoon Celtic salt
1/2 teaspoon fresh ground pepper
1 whole chicken, skinned and cut into serving pieces
1 13-ounce can coconut milk
3/4 cup purified water
1/4 cup fresh cilantro, finely chopped
1/4 cup green chile, finely chopped
1 pinch stevia
2 tablespoons chives, thinly sliced (optional)
sour cream (optional)

Melt coconut oil in a large pot on medium heat. Add onions and stir-fry until tender. Add garlic and ginger and cook until onions are lightly brown. Add curry powder, salt and pepper, while stirring continuously. Add chicken pieces and stir for three minutes. Cover and cook for 20 minutes, lifting lid occasionally to stir mixture. Stir in coconut milk and water. Cover and cook until tender. Add fresh cilantro, chile, stevia and cook for two more minutes. Garnish with sour cream and chives (optional).
Serves 4

Carbs per recipe: 23
Carbs per serving: 6

Garlic Lemon Chicken

1 whole chicken, cut into pieces
1 teaspoon garlic powder
1 teaspoon Celtic salt
1/2 teaspoon fresh ground pepper
6 garlic cloves, minced
3 tablespoons butter, melted
2 lemons, juiced

Season chicken with garlic powder, Celtic salt and fresh ground pepper. Place it on a broiler rack, with the skin portion facing up. Warm butter and add minced garlic cloves. Baste chicken liberally with lemon juice and garlic butter. Broil for about 12 minutes on one side. Turn, and again baste with lemon juice and garlic butter. Broil for 12 more minutes or until desired doneness (chicken is best when the juices run clear). Garnish with lemon slices and parsley sprigs.
Serves 4

Carbs per recipe: 18
Carbs per serving: 5

Chicken Vegetable Stir-fry

1 pound boneless, skinless chicken breasts
1 tablespoon coconut oil
1/4 cup onion, chopped
1 red pepper, diced
2 stalks celery, sliced
2 cups broccoli florets
1 can water chestnuts
2 cups mung bean sprouts

Marinade

3 tablespoons low-sodium soy sauce
1 tablespoon rice vinegar (unsweetened)
1 tablespoon purified water
3 garlic cloves, finely minced
1 1/2 ounces of fresh ginger, finely minced
1 pinch stevia

Cut chicken into bite-sized chunks and place in a medium bowl. Combine soy sauce, rice vinegar, water, garlic, ginger and stevia to make marinade. Pour liquid over chicken and allow to marinate for at least one hour, stirring constantly. Heat coconut oil in a large skillet over medium-high heat. Stir-fry sliced onion for about three minutes or until translucent. Drain chicken (set residual marinade aside), add it to the skillet, and stir-fry for five minutes. Add red pepper, celery and broccoli, water chestnuts and leftover marinade. Stir-fry for three minutes, add mung bean sprouts and stir-fry for two more minutes.
Serves 4

Carbs per recipe: 50
Carbs per serving: 13

Savory Roast Beef

1 beef roast (about 3 pounds)
8 garlic cloves, cut into small chunks
3 bay leaves, sliced
1 tablespoon butter, melted
1/2 teaspoon Celtic sea salt
1/8 teaspoon pepper, fresh ground

Place roast in a medium sized baking pan. Cut small slits over the surface of the entire roast and insert garlic chunks and bay leaf slices into them. Brush roast with melted butter and season with salt and pepper. Place roast in the oven and cook at 350 for about 90 minutes or until desired degree of tenderness.
Serves 6

Carbs per recipe: 7
Carbs per serving: 1

Meat Balls with Red Sauce

1 pound ground beef
1 egg, beaten
1/4 cup onion, minced
1 tablespoon Worcestershire sauce
1/4 teaspoon Italian spices
1/4 teaspoon garlic powder
1/4 teaspoon pepper
1 tablespoon coconut oil

Combine ground beef, beaten egg, onion, Worcestershire sauce, spices, garlic powder and pepper. Form into a large ball. Break off small pieces and shape these into one-inch balls. Melt coconut oil in a large skillet at medium heat and cook meat balls (turning as necessary) until golden brown.

Red Sauce

16 ounces of Italian stewed tomatoes,
chopped (no sugar added)
1/4 cup green pepper, finely minced
1 ounce fresh basil, minced
2 cloves garlic, minced
1 pinch stevia rebaudiana

Add stewed tomatoes, green pepper, basil, garlic and stevia to a medium pot over medium heat. Add (cooked) meatballs and simmer over medium-low heat for 20 minutes.
Serves 4

Carbs per recipe: 23
Carbs per serving: 6

Vegetable Beef Stir-Fry

1 pound beef (top round steak)
2 cups broccoli florets
1 cup zucchini, sliced
2 tablespoon low-sodium soy sauce
2 tablespoons dry sherry
1 pinch stevia
1 tablespoon coconut oil
1/2 cup water chestnuts, sliced
1 cup mung sprouts, sliced
3 garlic cloves, minced

Slice beef into thin bite-sized strips. If this is difficult, partially freeze it and slice across the grain. Meanwhile, steam broccoli and zucchini until lightly crisp. In a small bowl, mix soy sauce, sherry and stevia. Melt oil in a large skillet or wok over medium high heat. Stir-fry broccoli and zucchini until tender crisp (about two minutes).

Remove from heat, transfer to a bowl and add more oil if necessary. Return skillet to heat, add beef and stir-fry for about three minutes or until browned. Return broccoli and zucchini, along with soy sauce mixture, water chestnuts and mung sprouts. Stir-fry for two more minutes, turn off heat, add minced garlic, return cover and allow flavors to mingle for another minute before serving.
Serves 4

Carbs per recipe: 107
Carbs per serving: 27

Oven Steak with Vegetables

1 pound beef round steak,
cut 3/4 inch thick
1 tablespoon butter
Fresh ground pepper
1 small onion, chopped
1 cup canned tomatoes, sliced
1 teaspoon fresh dill, minced
2 medium yellow squash, sliced
2 medium zucchini, sliced

Cut steak into four serving-sized pieces. Melt butter in a large skillet on medium high and briefly brown meat for about one minute each side. Transfer steak to a large baking pan, retaining drippings in the skillet.

Sprinkle each side with fresh ground pepper to taste. Place chopped onion, tomatoes and dill into the same skillet and allow mixture to simmer for two minutes. Pour over meat and cook in the oven (covered) at 350. After 45 minutes of cooking, add sliced zucchini and squash. Replace lid and cook for 20 more minutes or until desired tenderness is achieved.
Serves 4

Carbs per recipe: 67
Carbs per serving: 17

Pepper Jack Melts

1 pound lean ground sirloin
1/4 cup sweet onion, finely chopped
1 teaspoon Worcestershire sauce
1/4 teaspoon garlic powder
1/8 teaspoon Tabasco sauce
1 pinch stevia
4 slices pepper jack cheese

Combine ground beef, onion, Worcestershire sauce, garlic powder, Tabasco sauce and stevia. Shape burgers into four five-inch patties and place them on a rack in a broiler pan. Broil burgers about three inches from the heat source for two to three minutes. Turn burgers just once, and broil the other side for one to two minutes.

Place one slice pepper jack cheese over each burger. Broil for one more minute. Remove from the oven and serve with lettuce, tomato and onion slices. Use Dijon mustard and mayonnaise as condiments.
Serves 4

Carbs per recipe: 8
Carbs per serving: 2

Grilled Rabbit

1 rabbit cut into serving pieces
1/2 cup apple cider vinegar
2 tablespoons purified water
4 garlic cloves, finely chopped
1 teaspoon Celtic salt
3 tablespoons butter, melted
2/3 cup whey protein concentrate, unflavored
1/2 teaspoon Celtic salt
1/2 teaspoon garlic powder
1/4 teaspoon pepper
1/8 teaspoon paprika

Place rabbit evenly in a shallow pan. Combine vinegar, water, garlic and salt and pour over meat pieces, allowing them to marinate for at least two hours.
Combine whey concentrate, salt, garlic powder, pepper and paprika. Remove meat from marinade and dip it into melted butter, coat it with whey mixture and transfer it to the grilling rack. Grill uncovered at 375 for 30 minutes or until fluids run clear.
Serves 4

Carbs per recipe: 10
Carbs per serving: 3

Moussaka

2 medium eggplants, cut into 1/4 inch slices
2 tablespoons coconut oil
1/2 cup onions, finely chopped
6 garlic cloves, minced
1 pound lamb meat, ground
2 tablespoon fresh oregano, minced
4 tablespoons fresh basil, minced
1 teaspoon fresh dill, minced
1/4 teaspoon fresh ground pepper
1 fresh, ripe tomato, chopped
1/2 cup butter
1 cup heavy cream
2 eggs, beaten
8 ounces feta cheese, finely crumbled

In a large skillet, melt oil on medium high. Stir-fry eggplant until tender and slightly browned. Remove from skillet and allow to drain. Reduce heat to medium and sauté onions in the same skillet until slightly tender. Add ground lamb, oregano, basil, dill and pepper, and stir continuously. When lamb begins to brown, remove form heat, add chopped tomatoes and minced garlic, stir, cover skillet and allow to sit . Meanwhile, melt butter in a small saucepan. Whisk in cream and beaten eggs and continue whisking mixture until evenly combined.

Preheat oven at 325. Cover a large casserole with a small amount of the egg-cream sauce. Layer with eggplant, lamb mixture, grated feta and sauce. Continue layering, and end with the egg-cream.

Serves 4

Carbs per recipe: 23
Carbs per serving: 6

Garlic Lamb Chops Marinade

2 tablespoons low-sodium soy sauce
2 tablespoons lemon juice
1 tablespoon Worcestershire sauce
4 garlic cloves, minced
2 tablespoon cilantro, chopped
1 pound lamb chops (about 3/4 inch)

Combine soy sauce with lemon juice, Worcestershire sauce, garlic and cilantro. Pour mixture over lamb chops and marinate in refrigerator for one hour. Remove lamb chops from the marinade and broil on high for five minutes on each side or until desired doneness.
Serves 4

Carbs per recipe: 41
Carbs per serving: 10

Other Ideas include tofu, pork recipes.

Vegetables

Spinach Sauté

1 tablespoon coconut oil
1 pound spinach, chopped
2 tablespoons low sodium soy sauce
2 garlic cloves, minced

Heat coconut oil in a medium-sized skillet over medium-high heat. Add chopped spinach and soy sauce, and stir-fry for about three minutes. Turn off heat, add minced garlic, stir and cover skillet for one or two minutes before serving.
Serves 4

Carbs per recipe: 21
Carbs per serving: 5

Steamed Vegetable Medley

1 cup broccoli florets
1 cup cauliflower, cut
1 cup zucchini, sliced
1 cup yellow squash, sliced

Wash and slice/cut broccoli florets, cauliflower, zucchini and yellow squash and place them in a steamer basket. Add 1/2 inch of water to the pot beneath the basket. Cover pot and steam vegetables on high heat for about six minutes or until vegetables are tender-crisp. Serve plain, with butter or with a tasty low-carb sauce (see Sauces). Serves 4

Carbs per recipe: 25
Carbs per serving: 6

Italian Zucchini Bake

4 small zucchini, thinly sliced
1/4 cup Parmesan cheese, finely grated
2 tablespoon fresh basil, minced
2 garlic cloves, minced
1/2 cup pizza seasoned tomato sauce
1/4 cup mozzarella cheese, grated

Place zucchini slices into an 8-inch casserole dish. Cover with Parmesan cheese and fresh basil. Mix tomato sauce and garlic and drizzle over zucchini. Cover and bake at 350 for 30 minutes or until vegetables are tender. Uncover and distribute grated mozzarella evenly over the top. Return to the oven (uncovered) and broil for two minutes or until cheese is melted and lightly golden.
Serves 2

Carbs per recipe: 41
Carbs per serving: 21

Ratatouille

1 tablespoon coconut oil
1/4 cup onion, chopped
2 garlic cloves, minced
1 cup eggplant, peeled and diced
1 green pepper, diced
1 cup zucchini, sliced
1 cup stewed tomatoes
1 tablespoon fresh basil, minced
1 tablespoon fresh parsley, minced
1/2 teaspoon oregano (dried)
1/2 teaspoon thyme (dried)

Melt coconut oil in a medium saucepan over medium heat. Add onion and garlic, and sauté until onions are translucent. Add eggplant, green pepper and zucchini, and stir-fry for four minutes or until vegetables are tender. Add stewed tomatoes, stir, cover and reduce heat to low. Simmer for 15 minutes. Then add basil, parsley, oregano and thyme. Simmer for 10 more minutes, stirring continuously.
Serves 4

Carbs per recipe: 45
Carbs per serving: 11

Vegetable Stir-fry

1 tablespoon coconut oil
2 tablespoons onion, chopped
1 cup mushrooms, sliced
1 cup green peppers, sliced
1 1/2 cups mung bean sprouts
2 tablespoons fresh ginger, thinly sliced
1 tablespoon low-sodium soy sauce
2 tablespoons sesame seeds, toasted

In a wok or skillet heat coconut oil over medium high heat. Add onion and stir-fry until light, translucent and soft. Add mushrooms, green peppers and stir-fry for about one minute. Add mung bean sprouts and stir-fry for one more minute. Add ginger and soy sauce and stir-fry for two more minutes or until vegetables are lightly tender. Top with toasted sesame seeds and serve.
Serves 4

Carbs per recipe: 27
Carbs per serving: 7

Mom's Famous Zucchini

Mom always intended to write a garlic cookbook — this is a family favorite, and this is as close as she got to a cookbook!

1 tablespoon coconut oil
1 medium onion, sliced
1 teaspoon thyme
1/2 teaspoon oregano
4 cups zucchini, sliced
4 garlic cloves, minced

Melt coconut oil in a large skillet over medium-high heat. Add onion, thyme and oregano, and sauté for two minutes or until onions are tender. Add zucchini and cook for five minutes, stirring constantly. If zucchini or onions begin sticking, add a small amount of water to the skillet. Once zucchini are tender, turn off the heat, add minced garlic, stir vegetables, cover skillet and allow to sit for one minute. Then serve immediately.
Serves 4

Carbs per recipe: 60
Carbs per serving: 15

Fragrant Steamed Artichokes

4 large artichokes
2 teaspoons Celtic salt
1 bay leaf
3 garlic cloves, sliced
5 peppercorns
1/4 lemon, thinly sliced

Wash artichokes, trim lower stalks, and remove hard outer leaves. Remove thorny pointed leaves by slicing about 1/6 off their tops. Pour water into a steaming pot and add bay leaf, garlic cloves, peppercorns, salt and lemon slices. Place pot over high heat and bring water to a boil. Place artichokes in the steaming basket with stem facing up. Steam for 30 to 45 minutes or until artichoke base is tender and outer leaves peel off easily. Remove artichokes and and serve with melted butter, flax oil with crushed garlic cloves or Hollandaise sauce (see Sauces).
Serves 4

Serve with: Melted butter or flax oil with fresh garlic cloves, crushed or Hollandaise sauce (see sauces).

Carbs per recipe: 52
Carbs per serving: 13

Amandine Asparagus

1 pound fresh asparagus
1/4 cup slivered almonds
1/4 cup butter
1 tablespoon lemon juice

Steam asparagus until tender crisp and set aside. In a medium-sized skillet over medium heat, toast slivered almonds until golden brown. Add butter and asparagus, and stir mixture gently for two to three minutes. Remove from heat and drizzle with lemon juice before serving.
Serves 4

Carbs per recipe: 13
Carbs per serving: 3

Sautéed Mung Sprouts

1 tablespoon coconut oil
1 medium onion, chopped
4 cups fresh mung sprouts
1 tablespoon low-sodium soy sauce
1 pinch stevia
1 teaspoon lemon juice
1/4 cup fresh basil, minced
2 garlic cloves, finely minced

Melt coconut oil in a medium skillet over medium heat. Sauté onions until tender. Turn heat up to medium-high. Add mung sprouts, soy sauce, stevia and lemon juice and stir fry for about two minutes or until sprouts are tender-crisp. Turn heat off, stir in minced basil and garlic, cover skillet and allow flavors to mingle for a few minutes before serving.
Serves 4

Carbs per recipe: 55
Carbs per serving: 14

Creamy Brussels Sprouts

1 pound brussels sprouts, trimmed
2/3 cup sour cream
3 tablespoons pimento, chopped
1 pinch stevia
salt and pepper to taste
paprika to taste
1/4 cup slivered almonds, toasted

Steam brussels sprouts for about 10 minutes. Place sour cream in a medium-sized pot and warm over medium heat. Add pimento, stevia, salt, pepper and brussels sprouts, while turning mixture gently with a fork. Remove from heat, transfer to a serving bowl and sprinkle lightly with paprika and toasted almonds before serving.
Serves 4

Carbs per recipe: 41
Carbs per serving: 10

Curried Cabbage

1 tablespoon coconut oil
1 small onion, finely chopped
4 cups green cabbage, finely chopped
1/2 cup zucchini, grated
1/4 cup coconut milk, boiling
1/8 cup coconut, grated (unsweetened)
1 tablespoon curry powder
1/8 teaspoon stevia
Celtic salt to taste
2 garlic cloves, minced

In a large skillet, melt coconut oil over medium heat. Sauté onion until tender, add cabbage and zucchini and continue to sauté, stirring occasionally. In a small bowl, mix boiling coconut milk, coconut, curry powder, stevia and salt. Add to vegetables and simmer until liquid is almost entirely cooked off. Turn heat off, add garlic cloves, stir, cover and allow to sit for one minute before serving.
Serves 4

Carbs per recipe: 59
Carbs per serving: 15

Gingered Chard

1 tablespoon coconut oil
1 one-inch chunk fresh ginger, sliced
2 bunches (about 1 pound) fresh chard, chopped
1 tablespoon low-sodium soy sauce
1 pinch stevia
1 teaspoon rice vinegar
1 tablespoon sesame seeds, toasted

Melt coconut oil in large skillet or wok over medium heat. Sauté ginger until tender.
Add chard, soy sauce, stevia and rice vinegar. Stir-fry until chard is tender and bright
green. Serve topped with toasted sesame seeds.
Serves 4

Carbs per recipe: 15
Carbs per serving: 4

Breads & Desserts

Soya Bread*

4 eggs, separated
1/4 cup sour cream
1/8 cup butter, melted
1/2 cup soy flour
1/3 cup Designer® Protein, natural flavor
2 teaspoons baking powder
Butter or coconut oil

Separate eggs and beat egg whites until they form stiff peaks. In a medium bowl, beat egg yolks, sour cream and melted butter. In a separate bowl, combine soy flour, Designer® Protein, and baking powder and beat into egg yolk mixture. Gently fold in egg whites. Pour batter into a buttered (or coconut oiled) nonstick bread loaf pan. Bake in a preheated oven at 350 for 45 minutes or until inserted toothpick comes out clean. Keeps fresh in refrigerator for about one week.
Makes 1 loaf
About 16 slices

Carbs per recipe: 19
Carbs per slice: 1

* Adapted from Dr. Atkins' New Diet Revolution

Peppered Cheese Bread

4 eggs, separated
1/4 cup sour cream
1/8 cup butter, melted
1/3 cup soy flour
1/3 cup Designer® Protein, natural flavor
2 teaspoons baking powder
1/2 cup peppered Jack cheese, grated (or use your favorite cheese)
Butter or coconut oil

Separate eggs and beat egg whites until they form stiff peaks. In a medium bowl, beat egg yolks, sour cream and butter. In a separate bowl, combine soy flour, Designer® Protein and baking powder. Beat flour combination into egg yolk mixture. Then alternatively fold in egg whites and grated cheese into batter. Pour into a buttered (or coconut oiled) nonstick bread loaf pan. Bake in a preheated oven at 350 for 45 minutes or until inserted toothpick comes out clean. Keeps fresh in refrigerator for about one week.
Makes 1 loaf
About 16 slices

Carbs per recipe: 20
Carbs per slice: 1

Sweet Almonds and Rutabaga

4 cups rutabaga, peeled and cubed
3 tablespoons butter
3/4 cup cream
1/2 teaspoon stevia
1/2 cup water
1 egg, beaten
1/4 cup slivered almonds, lightly toasted
Butter or coconut oil

Preheat oven at 300. Steam rutabagas until tender. Mash them and blend with butter, cream, stevia, water and egg. Transfer to a blender or food processor and whip until fluffy. Pour the mixture into a buttered (or coconut oiled) eight-inch baking pan. Bake for about 60 minutes or until toothpick comes out clean. Sprinkle with toasted almonds. Serves 4.

Carbs per recipe: 86
Carbs per serving: 22

"Pound Cake"

4 eggs, separated
1/4 cup butter, melted
1/2 teaspoon lemon zest
1 teaspoon vanilla
1/4 teaspoon stevia
2/3 cup Designer® Protein (French vanilla)
1/4 cup soy flour
2 teaspoons baking powder
Butter
nutmeg

Separate eggs and beat egg whites until they form stiff peaks. In a medium bowl, beat egg yolks, butter, lemon zest, vanilla and stevia. In a separate bowl, combine whey protein, soy flour and baking powder. Gently fold egg whites into batter. Pour mixture into a buttered nonstick bread loaf pan and lightly sprinkle with nutmeg. Bake in a preheated oven at 350 for 45 minutes or until inserted toothpick comes out clean. One loaf
About 12 medium slices

Carbs per recipe: 25
Carbs per serving: 2

Cinnamon Bran Muffins

3 eggs, separated
2 tablespoons butter, melted
2 tablespoons coconut oil, melted
1/2 cup Designer® Protein (French vanilla)
2 tablespoons soy flour
2 tablespoons wheat bran, toasted
1/4 cup walnuts, toasted
1/4 teaspoon ground cinnamon
1/8 teaspoon stevia
2 teaspoons baking powder
Butter

Separate eggs and beat egg whites until they form stiff peaks. In a medium bowl, beat egg yolks with butter and coconut oil. In a separate bowl, mix whey protein, soy flour, wheat bran, walnuts, cinnamon, stevia and baking powder. Beat dry mixture into egg yolk combination. Gently fold egg whites into batter and pour into a buttered nonstick muffin pan. Bake in a preheated oven at 350 for 30 minutes, or until inserted toothpick comes out clean.
Makes 8 muffins

Carbs per recipe: 27
Carbs per serving: 3

Coconut Pecan Meringues

4 egg whites
1/8 teaspoon stevia
1/2 teaspoon vanilla extract
1/3 cup Designer® Protein (French vanilla)
1/2 cup coconut, shredded and toasted (make sure it is unsweet-ened)
1/3 cup pecans, finely ground and toasted
Butter

In a medium bowl, beat egg whites, stevia extract and vanilla extract until stiff peaks form. In a small separate bowl, combine Designer protein, coconut and pecans. Gently fold nut mixture in with egg whites. Drop batter onto generously buttered cookie sheet by the heaping tablespoon. Bake at 250 for about 30 minutes. Turn oven off, keep oven door shut and allow cookies to remain in the oven for 30 more minutes.

Makes about 16 cookies

Carbs per recipe: 20
Carbs per serving: 1

Nutty Delights

3 egg whites
1/8 teaspoon stevia
1/2 cup Designer® Protein (French vanilla)
1/2 cup hazelnuts, finely ground and lightly toasted
Butter

In a medium bowl, beat egg whites and stevia extract until stiff peaks form. In a small separate bowl, combine Designer protein and ground, toasted hazelnut. Gently fold nut mixture in with egg whites. Drop batter onto generously buttered cookie sheet by the heaping tablespoon. Bake at 250 for about 30 minutes. Turn oven off, keep oven door shut and allow cookies to remain in the oven for 30 more minutes.

Makes about 12 cookies

Carbs per recipe: 26
Carbs per serving: 2

Whipped Topping

This creamy delight can be enjoyed as is or can be used to enhance many of your favorite low carb desserts.

1 cup heavy cream
1/2 teaspoon vanilla
1 dash stevia

In a medium-sized, chilled bowl, beat cream until almost thickened. Add vanilla and stevia. Beat until thick, soft peaks form. Enjoy over berries, with a favorite dessert or as a topping for low carb hot chocolate (see Beverages).
Makes 2 cups (32 tablespoons)

Carbs per recipe: 9
Carbs per 2 tablespoon serving: 1/2

Mia's Favorite Dessert

This simple recipe has remained my favorite dessert throughout the years.

1 cup strawberries
1 dash stevia
1/4 cup whipped topping
2 teaspoons coconut, shredded

Wash and slice berries, saving two whole berries as garnish. Pour 1/2 cup of berries into two dessert bowls and top with a dollop of stevia sweetened whipped topping. Place a whole berry on top, sprinkle with shredded coconut and enjoy.
2 servings

Carbs per recipe: 15
Carbs per serving: 8

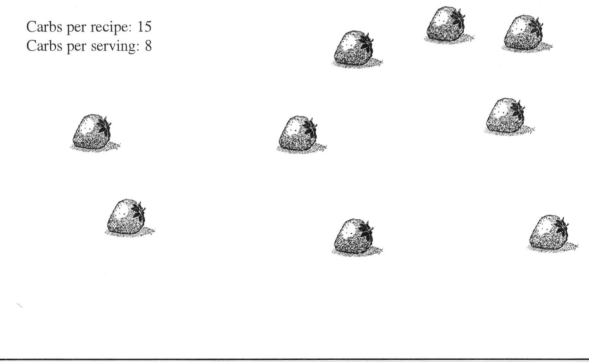

Designer Dessert

1/4 cup purified water
1 package gelatin
2/3 cup Designer® Protein (French vanilla)
1 cup purified water
1/2 cup cream
1/2 cup ice cubes
1/8 teaspoon stevia
1 teaspoon vanilla extract

In a small sauce pan, dissolve gelatin into water. Turn heat on low and stir mixture until gelatin is completely dissolved. Meanwhile, add whey protein, water, cream, ice cubes and vanilla extract to blender. Blend for one minute. Add gelatin water and blend for one more minute. Refrigerate and chill for about two hours.
4 servings

Carbs per recipe: 13
Carbs per serving: 3

Chocolate Strawberry Mousse

1/2 cup purified water
2 teaspoons gelatin
3 squares baker's chocolate (unsweetened), shredded
1/8 teaspoon teaspoon stevia extract
8 ounces heavy cream
1 teaspoon vanilla extract
1 cup fresh strawberries, sliced

Boil water and stir gelatin into boiling water until completely dissolved. Stir in shredded chocolate squares and stevia. In a small, chilled mixing bowl, beat cream until nearly thickened. Add vanilla and beat until peaks form. Gently fold in chocolate mixture and transfer into eight serving dishes, filling them only halfway. Add strawberry slices and cover with remaining mousse. Chill for at least one hour before serving. Serves 4

Carbs per recipe: 45
Carbs per serving: 11

Cottage Cheesecake

1 envelope Knox gelatin
1/4 cup purified water
1 egg yolk
1/3 cup heavy cream
1/3 cup purified water
1 teaspoon lemon zest (finely grated lemon rind)
1 cup cottage cheese
4 ounces cream cheese
1/2 teaspoon stevia
1 teaspoon lemon juice
1 teaspoon vanilla
2 tablespoons butter, melted
1/4 cup flax seeds, finely ground
1/4 cup almonds, finely ground
1 pinch stevia
1/4 teaspoon cinnamon
1/4 teaspoon nutmeg
1 egg white
1/2 cup heavy cream

Dissolve gelatin in 1/4 cup water. Set aside. Beat egg yolk with 1/3 cup cream and 1/3 cup water and place in a double boiler. Cook mixture over boiling water, gradually add gelatin water and continuing to stir as mixture thickens (about 10 minutes). Remove from heat and stir in lemon zest. Place cottage cheese and cream cheese with lemon juice, vanilla and stevia in a blender or food processor and blend until smooth.

continued on next page ...

Combine cheese mixture with gelatin mixture and place in refrigerator for about 15 minutes.

Meanwhile, make the crust by combining melted butter with ground flax seeds, almonds, stevia, cinnamon and nutmeg. Spread and press this into the bottom of a nine-inch pie plate. Beat egg white until stiff peaks form and whip cream until soft peaks form. Alternately fold these into the cooled cheese mixture until evenly combined. Pour this into a pie plate and refrigerate.
Makes one 9-inch pie
8 servings

Carbs per recipe: 47
Carbs per serving: 6

Strawberry Cream Treats

4 ounces whipped cream cheese, softened
1/8 teaspoon almond extract
2-3 dashes stevia
1 1/3 cups strawberries, sliced

Beat cream cheese with almond and stevia, saving a small dollop for garnish. Transfer evenly into four custard cups. Combine strawberry slices with stevia and place over cream cheese mixture. Garnish with a small dollop of cream cheese mixture in the center and place a whole strawberry in the center. Chill for three hours and serve. Serves 4

Carbs per recipe: 19
Carbs per serving: 5

Flax-Nut Pie Crust

1/4 cup flax seeds, finely ground
3 tablespoons ice water
1/2 teaspoon vinegar
3/4 cup almonds, finely ground
1 dash stevia
1/4 teaspoon salt
1 tablespoon coconut oil, melted

Soak ground flax seeds in water and vinegar for at least 15 minutes. Stir these together and set aside. In a separate bowl, mix ground almonds with stevia, salt and melted coconut oil. Combine seed and nut mixture and stir until evenly mixed. Transfer into a nine-inch pie pan, pressing evenly along the bottom and edges. Prick crust with a fork and bake for 15 minutes at 325. Allow crust to cool before adding filling.

Carbs per recipe: 49

Creamy Blueberry Pie

8 ounces cream cheese, softened
1/4 cup purified water
2-3 dashes stevia
1 teaspoon vanilla
1 tablespoon cream
3/4 cup purified water
1 tablespoon cornstarch
1 tablespoon fresh lemon juice
1/8 teaspoon stevia
1 pound fresh or frozen blueberries (unsweetened)

Mix cream cheese with water, stevia, vanilla and cream. If using frozen blueberries, drain fluid and use the liquid in place of water. Spoon cream cheese mixture into pie crust (pie pan if not using crust) and chill. In a medium-sized pot, combine water, cornstarch, lemon juice and stevia. Cook and stir over medium heat until thickened. Remove from heat and stir in blueberries and lemon juice. Allow berry mixture to cool, then spoon over chilled cream cheese mixture. Chill pie for at least two hours and garnish with whipped topping (optional) just before serving.
Serves 12

Carbs per recipe: 55
Carbs per serving: 5

Coconut Cream Dream

1/3 cup purified water
1 packet gelatin
1 13-ounce can coconut milk, with carbohydrate portion (clear \liquid) removed
1/3 cup whey protein concentrate, vanilla flavor
1/4 cup cream
1/4 cup grated coconut
1/4 teaspoon stevia

Add gelatin to water in a small saucepan. Turn heat on low and gently stir gelatin in water until completely dissolved. Pour coconut milk, whey protein concentrate, cream, stevia and half of the grated coconut into a blender or food processor. Blend for 30 seconds. Add gelatin water and blend for 30 more seconds. Pour into four custard cups, sprinkle with remaining grated coconut and chill until dessert sets. Serve cold with a dollop of whipped topping.
Serves 4

Carbs per recipe: 9
Carbs per serving: 2

Tofu Mocha Supreme

12 ounces silken, soft tofu
3 tablespoons cocoa powder
1 1/2 teaspoons instant decaf granules
1/8 teaspoon stevia powder
2 tablespoons flax oil
1 teaspoon vanilla extract

Blend tofu, cocoa powder, decaf, stevia, flax oil and vanilla extract in a food processor or blender until smooth. Transfer into four custard cups. Chill for at least an hour before serving
Serves 4

Carbs per recipe: 18
Carbs per serving: 5

Strawberry Cheesecake Treats

4 ounces cream cheese
1/8 teaspoon stevia powdered extract
1 cup heavy cream, whipped
1/2 cup strawberries, sliced

Beat cream cheese and stevia until thoroughly combined. Fold in whipped cream.
Place into four small dessert bowls and garnish with sliced strawberries.
Serves 4

Carbs per recipe:
Carbs per serving:

Easy Strawberry Tiramisu

1 cup ripe strawberries, washed and sliced
1/4 cup rum
8 slices "pound cake" (see Baking)
4 tablespoons cream cheese
4 teaspoons espresso
Cocoa powder

Pour one tablespoon of rum into four small dessert bowls. Place one slice of "pound cake" over the rum. Spread one tablespoon of cream cheese onto each portion, and cover with equal amounts of sliced strawberries. Cover strawberries with a second slice of "pound cake" and drizzle each one with a teaspoon of espresso. Lightly dust with cocoa powder and allow to sit for one hour before serving.
4 servings

Carbs per recipe: 32
Carbs per serving: 8

Sweet Raspberry Pie

A rich dessert that is as delicious as it is easy to make.

1 tablespoon butter
1 tablespoon flax meal, finely ground
1 1/2 pounds ricotta cheese
3 eggs
1/4 teaspoon stevia
1 teaspoon vanilla extract
1/2 cup fresh raspberries
1//4 cup slivered almonds, toasted

Grease a glass nine-inch pie dish with soft butter. Spread a fine, even layer of flax meal over the bottom and sides of the dish. Place ricotta, eggs, stevia and vanilla in a blender or food processor and blend until smooth. Add berries and gently mix these in with a spoon. Transfer to the pie dish, swirl the top, and bake for 40 minutes at 400. Remove pie, sprinkle with toasted almonds and bake for 10 more minutes or until tooth pick comes out clean from the center. Cool and serve.
Serves 8

Carbs per recipe: 34
Carbs per serving: 4

Chocolate Coconut Pudding

1/4 cup cool, purified water
1 package gelatin
2/3 cup (2 scoops) Designer® Protein (French vanilla)
3/4 cup purified water
1/2 cup coconut milk
1/4 cup cream
4 tablespoons cocoa powder
1/2 cup ice cubes
1/8 teaspoon stevia
1 teaspoon vanilla
1 tablespoon coconut, shredded (unsweetened)

In a small sauce pan, dissolve gelatin in water. Turn heat on low and stir until gelatin is completely dissolved. In the meantime, add whey protein, water, coconut milk, cream, cocoa powder, ice cubes and vanilla to blender. Blend for one minute. Add gelatin water and blend for one more minute. Sprinkle with shredded coconut, refrigerate and chill for about two hours before serving
4 servings

Carbs per recipe: 22
Carbs per serving: 6

Appendix A
Low Carb Shopping List

The following shopping list will help you restock your kitchen cupboards. Have fun with this, and be sure to focus on the foods you like to eat and cook with!

Vegetables
All leafy greens and related, including:
arugula, baby lettuce mix, beet greens, bok choy, chard, collard greens, endive, escarole, green cabbage, green leaf lettuce, kale, Napa cabbage, red leaf lettuce, romaine lettuce, spinach

All non-starchy vegetables, including: alfalfa sprouts, asparagus, avocado, broccoli, brussels sprouts, cauliflower, celery, cucumber, eggplant, green beans, jicama, kohlrabi, leeks, mung bean sprouts, mushrooms, okra, onions, purple cabbage, radish, rhubarb, scallions, snow pea pods, summer squash, tomato, turnips, zucchini squash

Canned or condiment vegetables, including: artichoke hearts (in oil or water), bamboo shoots, hearts of palm, olives (all varieties), pickles (unsweetened only), sauerkraut, water chestnuts

All salad herbs, including: basil, chicory, chives, cilantro, dill, fennel, garlic, oregano, parsley, rosemary, thyme.

Low carb, low glycemic fruits: strawberries, blueberries, raspberries*
* In the beginning of the LCAA Diet, these are best consumed in 1/4 to 1/2 cup servings

Meats:
Coleman and other organic or free-range beef, lamb, pork, veal, venison and other wild game
Exceptions: no processed meats containing sugars and/or nitrates or other carbohydrates.

Fish: all fish, especially cold water fish (rich in omega-3 fatty acids. Exceptions: processed fish or fish with nitrites or nitrates. Avoid imitation crab, lobster or other imitation fish

Fowl: all organic or free-range varieties, including chicken, Cornish game hen, turkey and goose. Exceptions: no processed poultry or products containing nitrites, nitrates, sugars or other carbohydrates.

Dairy: Organic or free range eggs, cream, kefir (0-1 gm carbohydrate per serving), sour cream, cheeses*, whey protein concentrate (Next Nutrition™, Designer Protein®)

*Carbohydrate content should be 1 gm or less per one-ounce serving

Vegan protein sources: Tofu, tofu flour, soy flour, low carb soy powder, tofu cheese, rice or soy cheese (check carbohydrate content), tofu sausages, texturized vegetable protein (TVP), Smart Dogs or other low carb soy "hot dogs." Most of these products have a very low carbohydrate content. Always check labels before buying.

Condiments: Horseradish, mayonnaise, mustard, Tabasco sauce, Worcestershire Sauce

Smoothie mixes: Whey protein concentrate, soy protein powder or other low carb protein powders

Oils and fats: Whole avocado, coconut milk, coconut oil, butter, flax oil*, hemp oil*, pumpkin seed oil*, olive oil*, all nut*, seed*, and vegetable* oils are allowed. Mayonnaise is allowed, unless you are on a yeast-restricted diet.

*Do not heat these, as it destroys their nutritional value.

Best oils and fats for cooking: coconut oil, palm kernel oil and butter. These are naturally solid at room temperature, are able to withstand heat and are therefore best to cook and bake with.
Fats to avoid: all margarine, shortening and trans fatty acids (see chapter x)

Beverages: Herb tea, green tea, broth or bullion, lemon or lime juice as flavoring (1.4 gm carbohydrate per tablespoon), seltzer water, mineral water, club soda, cream, naturally flavored water.

Sweeteners: Non-caloric herbal sweeteners, including stevia white extract, stevia herbal powder and stevia liquid extracts.

Sugars and synthetic sweeteners to avoid:
Sugars include all refined sugars and syrups: most products ending with -ose:
glucose (dextrose), fructose, levulose, galactose. Double sugars: sucrose (table sugar), maltose (in beer) and lactose (in milk). Syrups made from sugar cane, sugar beets, rice, barley, sorghum, honey and maple.

Synthetic sweeteners, including aculfame K, saccharin and aspartame (Nutrasweet) should be avoided, since sufficient evidence suggests they may be hazardous to health.

Appendix B
Resources for Quality Low-Carb Products

For low carbohydrate shakes, ketosis sticks, bake mixes and other valuable resources:
Atkins Nutritionals Inc.
185 Oser Ave.
Hauppauge, N.Y. 11788
(800) 628--5467

For Whey Protein Concentrate
Next Proteins™:Designer Protein®: Highest quality whey protein concentrate (WPC)
P.O. Box 2469
Carlsbad, Calif. 92018
800-GOT-NEXT

For Soy Protein Concentrate
Next Proteins™: ISIS™ soy protein (free of genetically modified soybeans)
P.O. Box 2469

Carlsbad, Calif. 92018
800-GOT-NEXT

For Organic Produce
CSA: Community-Supported Agriculture (Groups that contract area farmers who agree to grow organic produce)
Robyn Van En Center for CSA Resources
(717) 264-4141 ext. 3247 or

Biodynamic Farming and Gardening Association
(800) 516-7797

For Organic Beef
Coleman Beef

For Celtic Ocean Sea Salt
The Grain & Salt Society
273 Fairway Drive
Asheville, N.C. 28805
(800) TOP SALT (867-7258)